A Play and Its Parts

A Play

GERALD WEALES

and Its

Basic Books, Inc., Publishers

Parts

New York

CULTURE &

DISCOVERY

For THE MORRISONS

To be passed
from Donnie
to Debbie
to David
to Andrew Gerald
to Jeremy

Contents

A Play and Its Parts

I

The World's a Stage

I stood at my back door and watched a child playing in the neighboring yard. A boy of two with a sizeable vocabulary which he seldom uses, he was involved in a number of complicated operations in which he used gestures and gibberish to carry on important conversations with his dog, a rosebush, a slightly decayed plastic football, and a stopped-up drain. There was intensity and purpose in each one of his communications; the former was easy to see, the latter was apparent but unknowable. I spoke his name and, in doing so, intruded my presence into the private worlds that he had been constructing for his own use. He turned and began to run up and down the yard, performing a special act for me. His body, his manner, his way of moving expressed both pride and shyness. He watched me out of the corner of his eye to make sure that I was watching him and that I was impressed. I said a few words to assure him that I was indeed watching and impressed, and then I went back inside and left him to the dog, the bush, the football, and the drain.

In describing this incident I have used a number of words—*playing, performing, act, gesture*—which one uses automatically in talking about the theater and about plays. Of course, these words have diverse and often complicated meanings; they are used for actions which have little to do with the stage. Still, the same words can be used to describe what goes on in life and what goes on in the fictional world of the theater. One reason is that there is a close connection between the two. "All the world's a stage," says Jaques in Shakespeare's *As You Like It*, "And all the men and women merely players." Jaques fancies himself something of a philosopher, so he goes on to explain that "one man in his time plays many parts" and to describe the seven ages—from infancy to old age—which are the main "acts" in each man's repertory of characters. Antonio in *The Merchant of Venice* says much the same thing; he is feeling sorry for himself, however, so his remarks are more personal than those of Jaques:

> I hold the world but as the world, Gratiano—
> A stage, where every man must play a part,
> And mine a sad one.

Gratiano, partly to cheer up his friend, partly because the role does fit his personality, says, "Let me play the fool." The comparison between the world and the stage comes naturally to the lips of Shakespeare's characters, as naturally as to your own when you say to a friend, "Stop it! You're just putting on an act."

What Shakespeare recognized in his choice of metaphor, what psychologists recognize when they talk about role-playing, what most of us admit if we stop to think about it for a minute, is that all of us are acting all the time. What is more, most of the time we know it. Take my two-year-old neighbor. Each of the little scenes which he played was a game of *let's-pretend* which involved only one conscious performer. In a way, each of his actions was a small play. I assume that, for the length of his conversation, the rosebush, say, had acquired a particular personality, and he had put on one to match it or contrast to it, to plead with it or dominate it. I have no idea of what his little plays were about and no way of finding out. All children invent invisible playmates, animate inanimate objects, humanize dogs and cats, but as soon as an adult breaks into the fantasy, the child changes it or erases it. What happens, of course, is that a new play begins, one in which the child becomes something in relation to the intruding adult. When I called my neighbor by name, the rosebush became a rosebush once again, and he became a fabulous runner, someone or something moving at an incredible and admirable speed. His movement was a bid for my attention and my applause. As soon as he responded to my voice, I ceased to be an unseen observer and became the audience he expected me to be; the words that I spoke before I went back inside were the applause that his act demanded. I had played my part, too.

As we grow up, we tend to quit playing the fantasy games of childhood. They move inside our heads, and it is there that we imagine ourselves heroes or victims in little dramas in which we write everyone's lines. Anyone who tries to play his fantasy in the open (that man you sometimes see in the street holding an intense conversation with himself) is considered a little mad, unless he (or more often she) has a dog or cat or bird to play the other part. Not that overt play-acting stops with adulthood. It simply changes its character (and its characters). We begin to perform in little scenes with other people, scenes in which we wear our own names and our opposites wear theirs. Consider the short, short play which follows:

Scene: Outside Any High School, Anyville, USA
Cast of Characters: Patsy (age 15)
                          Myrna (age 15)
                          David (age 15½)
                          Mr. Kristol (age 47), math teacher

Patsy *is standing on the walk outside the high school.*
Myrna *enters.*

Patsy: Hi, Myrna.

Myrna: Hi, Patsy. How's everything today?

Patsy: I feel lousy. How's yourself?

Myrna: Me? I'm a positive spazz. See you inside.

      (Myrna *exits.* Mr. Kristol *enters.*)

Mr. K.: Good morning, Patsy. How do you feel this lovely morning?

Patsy: Just fine, Mr. Kristol. Just fine. How about you, sir?

Mr. K.: Just fine, Patsy. Just fine.

      (Mr. Kristol *exits smiling. Enter* David.)

David: Hi, Patsy.

Patsy: Hi, Dave.

David: How's everything?

Patsy: Oh, I don't know. Why do you ask?

David: Oh, I don't know. I thought maybe I'd come over tonight and play you my new record. It's Fats Onthefire singing "Chik-chak-chok-chuk, I love you, baby, chuk-chok-chak-chik."

Patsy: Crazy.

(*Exit* Patsy *and* David *together, into school.*)

Since Patsy is at the center of this little scene, we can see her changing with each encounter, but any scene, however casual, involves a mutual performance. There is no reason to suppose that Myrna, David, and Mr. Kristol have not also just passed through a series of brief scenes in which what they said and the way they said it depended in part on whom they were speaking to. Consider an ordinary day in the life of an ordinary high school boy. In the course of twelve or fourteen hours, he has to be a son to his parents, a performance that is complicated by the fact that he is a different son to his mother than he is to his father and further by the fact that what is expected from him at the breakfast table is not the same as that expected at the dinner table. He may have to be a big brother or a little brother, or both, a performance that changes according to the size, sex, and situation of the creature to whom he must be brotherly—whether he has to protect a little sister or torture a little brother. He will have to be a student to a string of different teachers, and his performance in each class depends not only on the subject but on the teacher and the teacher's own interest in the boy, the subject, the school, and the mortgage on his house. He will have to be one of the boys, a performance that changes according to what the group is doing (studying in the classroom, telling dirty stories in the locker room, playing scrub football on the school lawn) and also according to whether he is in or out of any particular group. He will have to be a boy to the girls in his class, a performance that changes with each girl, that depends not only on his interest in or indifference to any one girl, but on his own idea—and his guess at the girl's opinion—of himself as a ladies' man. He will probably be a customer to a number of businessmen—in drug stores, groceries, sandwich shops—and his performance as a customer changes according to whether the person waiting on him is a stranger, a friend, or an acquaintance and whether what he is buying is something he wants or something that he thinks someone else thinks he ought to want. If he has a job, he will be an employee to a boss and his performance will change according to how well or how badly he is doing his job that day and how his employer feels about his success or failure. He is likely also to be a friend, an enemy, a stranger, a casual acquaintance, his father's son (not to his father but to someone who knows his father), a master (if he has a dog), an eater, a drinker. The list is endless. Not only does he play a wide variety of roles during the day, but within the roles there are variations which depend on how other people act and respond.

For the most part these performances are automatic. We shift easily from one role to another. There are set situations with pat lines which all of us know. Ordinarily, when someone says, "How are you?," he does not really want to know how you are. He simply wants you to give him the stock answer, "O.K. And you?" Still, formal exchange, however empty, is a useful convention, for it would be a bit difficult to concentrate on our lines all the time. We can save our really important performances for those scenes from which we hope to get something—a kiss, a job, a loan. Our success in any such scene is a kind of applause, although it is given, in this case, by a fellow performer, not by an outside audience. Often, however, an outside audience is an important consideration. A quarrel between two brothers may be for a parent's eye (the applause comes when the parent chooses sides); a private conversation may really be for an eavesdropper (the applause comes when what is overheard is repeated and one's social stock goes up).

In any scene, casual or complicated, one's performance is controlled by two or three things which work together or in conflict. To begin with, there is the general role that the occasion demands. Let's take, as an example, a young man attempting to explain to his father—who has already refused him once—why the young man's need for the automobile that night is so much greater than the father's. The general role is *son*. The variation on the general role is one that involves a strong sense of responsibility (he will see that nothing happens to the car and get it back at a certain time) and of status (everyone else will be driving). The young man's interpretation of both the general role and the variation depends on his knowledge of the father, on his having decided, from past scenes, that the father feels thus and so about the father–son relationship, about responsibility, and about status. Up to that point, the young man can operate without too much difficulty. He can come into the room with his pitch planned. Chances are he will have worked it out before he approaches the father, will have provided lines for himself and his father, a small dialogue in which he is finally persuasive. The difficulty, in practice, of course is that the father has not read the script. If he happens to give the right lines, the young man may indeed be triumphant in the way he planned. If the wrong lines come, the young man will have to modify his performance to fit the new situation, and his success probably depends finally on his ability to keep control of the scene. If he is right in his interpretation of the father, his chances are good even if the lines are wrong. But if something has happened that day to make the father decide that all sons are ingrates, juvenile delinquents, and status-ridden snobs, the young man may find himself playing in the father's scene and not in his own. He may not only not get the car, he may get the hell bawled out of him as well.

"This above all," Polonius tells Laertes in *Hamlet*, just before the young man sets out to study in Paris, "to thine own self be true." This line comes at the end of Polonius' long and very famous speech on behavior which says, in effect, "Behave according to a set of sensible maxims, be the son I want you to be." It has little to do with whatever *self* there is in Laertes. In fact, whenever anyone says in exasperation, "Oh, be yourself," he probably means that he wishes you would be whatever he thinks you are or ought to be. It is the multiplicity of selves in any man that makes him interesting. With such riches in a tiny body, it is not surprising that we have developed a habit of day-to-day acting in which we modify our personality to fit the immediate demands of a social, economic, or psychological situation. We know the way certain characters behave (football heroes, for instance, or policemen, or girls in love) and, if the occasion demands, we can recognize—even become—that character. Some people believe that we are only the sum of all the selves dictated to us by the situations through which we pass. Some people believe that there is an essential, probably a secret self, our true reality which remains hidden from almost everyone, sometimes even ourselves. In any case, Jaques is right; we are on stage all the time.

That may be why the theater and all its related forms (movies, television) fascinate us so.

2
The Play

There are almost as many ways of looking at the drama as there are people who write books about it. One of the simplest and most useful ways of approaching dramatic production is to consider a play as an extension of the kind of day-to-day acting described in the first chapter. It is an extension in which an order is imposed on what is accidental and uncontrollable in the real world. One of the functions of art—and the making of a play is an art, or a combination of several arts—is such an imposition of order: the giving of meaning to what is vague, of form to what is formless, of boundaries to what is continuous. The difference between an actual situation and a play, of course, is that the playwright controls the play from the outside, while anyone involved in a situation attempts and, for the most part, fails to control the situation from the inside.

Insofar as a character in a play is concerned, however,

a play is a situation. In that fact lies half the fun. I suppose I should have used a more exalted word than *fun*, should have said *artistic experience* or something like that, but there is a great deal too much unnecessary solemnity about art. Too many people see plays and read books and look at pictures because they are convinced it is good for them, like eating roughage or taking vitamins.

Part of the pleasure of seeing a play lies in the fact that the character behaves as though he were in a situation in which the part he plays depends only on himself and the demands of the other characters. Since such a circumstance is the one we regularly find ourselves in in ordinary life, it is possible for us to sympathize with the character, perhaps even to identify with him in his efforts. This is the first, the most obvious response to a play, the one made by the sentimental lady who begins to cry in the darkened movie theater when the heroine goes blind—Bette Davis in *Dark Victory* or Susan Hayward in *Stolen Hours*. But it is only half the fun. We, as members of the audience, not only stand with the characters, but with the playwright. Our pleasure in the play is not simply that of being moved by the characters in action, but of seeing the over-all pattern, of getting the playwright's point.

Take, for example, Anton Chekhov's play *The Sea Gull.* One of the leading characters is a young man named Treplev who wants, among other things, to impress his mother. The mother, Arkadina, is a famous actress who does not mind playing at being a mother once in a while, but who is really preoccupied with herself, as most actors are (in fact, as most people are). In the first act of Chekhov's play, Treplev is putting on a play that he has written, a very abstract play full of IDEAS and without human characters. Insofar as we sympathize with Treplev, we want his play to be a success; we want Arkadina to applaud, to embrace Treplev, to call him son and playwright. When the play is repeatedly interrupted by comments, Treplev becomes angry, stops the production, denounces his mother and runs off to pout. In a way, he has our sympathy, but it is not quite as easy as those crying ladies in the movie make it sound. There are playwrights who want the audience to identify with just one character, to suffer with him and for him, but their plays are usually superficial, good for a tear and not much more. The best playwrights—and Chekhov is one of the best—make it more difficult for the audience.

In the scene above, even while we sympathize with Treplev, something in us is on the side of Arkadina. She is, after all, an actress who is beginning to get old and who has a grown son whose presence continually reminds her of the fact. Besides that, the kind of play that Treplev has written is a direct attack on the kind of play Arkadina acts in, a way of telling her that she and all that she has been doing all her life is silly and shallow and meaningless. Her disruption of his play grows out of her need to protect herself as a woman and as a professional performer, and certainly anyone ought to be able to sympathize with an act of self-defense. To complicate matters further, the stage is crowded with a group of people, each of whom—like Treplev and Arkadina—is trapped by his own frustrations and his own dreams. If half our mind, half our allegiance, is up there on stage, acting with first one, then another, of the characters, the other half is standing off with Chekhov, seeing that stage full of characters from a vantage point that lets us know that the sum of all their struggles to assert themselves is Chekhov's idea of, and comment on, life—his recognition that it is almost impossible for two people ever to communicate with each other, and his acceptance that this situation is at once funny and painful.

The double response that I described above, that of being both inside and outside a play at once, is a sophisticated one, but it is not an uncommon one. There are a number of familiar phrases, however, which suggest otherwise. We say that someone is "drawn into a play" or that he "lost himself in the action." Some playwrights and actors might like to think that this is possible because what a compliment it would be to their writing or their acting to have an audience actually forget itself. Of course, that would be hypnotism, not art. Bertolt Brecht, the German playwright, was convinced that, in the ordinary theatrical situation, the audience is swept away and loses all its critical faculties. Since he wanted his audiences to think about the subjects of his plays, to contemplate action that might bring about social change, he was in favor of special techniques of acting and production which would remind the audience that it was in a theater. He has had a wide influence on contemporary theater because people on both sides of the footlights have been fascinated by some of his devices. Still, there is something wrong with his first assumption. Surely, phrases like *drawn in, swept away, lost himself in* more accurately describe a state of excitement than they do a loss of self-identification. There is a story told about a man in one of the Western mining camps who, having never seen a play before, decided that the heroine was really in danger and shot the villain. Such innocence is rare. Even the young boy at the cowboy movie, anxiously gripping the back of the seat in front of him, knows that the posse is going to get there on time. The boy is not only identifying with the hero, trapped and fighting desperately, but he is also himself, and in that role he knows how the cowboy movie works as an art form. To be both moved by a performance and aware of it as a performance at the same time is probably the greatest pleasure one can have in the theater.

Although I have been talking about the theater (and occasionally movies) in the paragraphs above, it should be remembered that the response I have been describing is not peculiar to the dramatic arts. Something similar happens when one looks at a painting or reads a novel. When I look at one of Renoir's picnic scenes, part of me at least wants to climb into the frame and join those lovely ladies in all that comforting green while the other part is aware that the picture is a balance of color, line, movement. When I read Henry Fielding's *Tom Jones*, part of me is caught up in the story, tramping along with Tom from one adventure to the next, while the other part of me is aware that Fielding's digressions are not really intrusions, that the novel is a total statement growing out of an interaction of story and comment. In one sense, then, the various arts elicit similar responses. Still, each art has its own character, its own way of working, and if we are to understand the play and how it functions, we will have first to separate it from the other arts.

There is a tendency these days—in colleges at least—to teach literature by genres, to divide courses into sections on prose (fiction and nonfiction), poetry, and drama. Such a division tells one of the truths about drama, that it is a literary genre. It is an important truth. For the written word is the basic material for the play, just as it is for the poem or the novel. The big difference between the play and the other literary forms is that the play is conceived not to be read, but to be seen and heard in the theater. For this reason, the playwright can draw on the nonverbal arts to achieve what he wants in his play. Poetry and fiction sometimes get musical effects in the way the words are marshalled; sometimes they call up pictures. The play can bring in music, bring in pictures (the sets, say) and use them to replace words. Where a novelist may describe a gesture that one of his characters makes, and the description may be important to the whole point of the novel, the playwright can call on an actor to make the gesture; the description becomes unnecessary. The play, then, is a nonliterary as well as a literary form.

There is a quarrel that has been going on for years between two groups who should be friends and allies since both are lovers of plays. On one side there are those who speak of dramatic literature with the emphasis on *literature*, who talk of the play as though it were only a brother to the novel and the poem and not a theatrical form at all. On the other side there are those who would swallow the word *literature* if they ever let themselves use a phrase like *dramatic literature;* they treat the play as though it were only a brother to those mute forms, the dance and the mime, and not a literary form at all. In this book, I will try to walk a fine line between the two sides.

In its final form, when it is given flesh on a stage, the play is a collaborative effort in which director, actors, designer, sound engineer, and the other technicians join the playwright to create the finished product. Often an actor or director with a strong personality will steal a play away from the playwright, turn it into a vehicle for self-advertisement. Such a production can be amusing to watch, but it is not exactly what I think of as a play; it is a little like an art gallery in which the owner has removed the artist's paintings from the frames and substituted photographs of himself. The play on stage should be an embodiment of the play on the page. The playwright—his conception and his creation—

should be the heart of the theatrical production. Edward Albee, praising Alan Schneider, who has directed many of his plays, says, "Alan's great virtue is this: His main concern is with getting the playwright's work on the stage the way the playwright intended it." Since Albee is a playwright, the testimonial may sound as though he were looking after his own interests, but, in this case, self-interest happens to be also the interests of the art form. In the theater at its best, the play's the thing, and the play is the thing that the playwright writes.

This emphasis on the playwright is one way of differentiating between the play and the other major acted art form, the film. From time to time, I will refer to movies for examples to clarify a particular device that a playwright has used, but it is a good idea to remember that there are essential differences between a play and a film, as vital as those between a play and a novel. The play is performed by live actors on a three-dimensional stage; the film by photographic images on a two-dimensional screen. The play is anchored to a limited space, a never-changing distance from our seats; in the film, the camera can bring the action directly to us (in close-ups) or push it into the barely visible distance. The most important difference, however, is that the film, for all that it makes use of words, is finally a series of visual images, and it is the organizer of those images—the director, ideally—who is the creative center of the movie as the playwright is of the play. The television play falls somewhere between the movie and the play, but—although it is very restricted when one considers what can be done in a movie—it is probably more like the film than it is like the play.

In the chapters that follow, we will consider the way plays work, which means that we will consider not only those elements—plot, character, language—which are the play-

wright's special province, but those tools—sets, lights, costumes—which he has learned to borrow from the performer.
I will have to go to printed plays to find examples to illustrate
the points I want to make. I once appeared on a panel with
two eminent directors who got carried away with their allegiance to the play on stage and insisted that there was no
such thing as a play on the printed page—that nothing
existed. What they were really saying, of course, is that they
did not trust the reader's imagination. If we really believed
those two men, we would condemn ourselves to an almost
playless existence. Even in a city like New York, where there
is a great deal of theater, the available produced plays are few
in number compared to the vast dramatic literature; in most
cities and towns, a man would be lucky to see two or three
plays a year. Fortunately, the two directors overstate the
case. The play, ideally, is a thing seen on stage. In a pinch,
we can read it and let our imaginations stage it in our heads.
There are books enough that tell you how to direct, act, dress,
and light amateur theatricals. The chapters that follow are
supposed to be of use in those mental productions that make
a stage of the page.

3

So What Happened?

According to Aristotle, art is primarily an imitation of men in action. In the two thousand years since Aristotle gave his lectures on tragedy, the theater has undergone a wide variety of changes, but, in most cases, plays are still organized around an action. The first question one asks of a play is: What happens in it? Sometimes the question reads differently: What's it about? Although the two questions are not really the same—what a play is about is not necessarily what happens in it—both questions, asked casually, are likely to be answered by a recounting of the plot.

There are a number of words that are commonly used to indicate what happens in a play: *story, plot, action*. The meanings of these words are not completely clear; sometimes they are treated as synonyms, sometimes they are supposed to indicate separate but related things. There is no point in attempting precise definitions here because, whenever you read a book about the theater, you will have to adjust to the writer's particular usage. Still, a few remarks need not be too confusing. *Story* is a word that indicates in the most general way what happens in a play. The story of John Millington Synge's *The Playboy of the Western World* involves an ineffectual young man who turns into "a likely gaffer," as he says, when an Irish village makes a hero of him for a crime he is supposed to have committed. The story of Noël Coward's *Blithe Spirit* recounts the unsuccessful attempts of a ghost to kill her former husband so that he can join her in what she calls "the other side." The story of Sophocles' *Oedipus Rex* is the king's discovery that he is the man whose crime has brought a plague to his city.

Plot is like *story*, but it implies not only what happens, but the order in which things happen. The *plot* of the play is the whole pattern of events. The plot of *Oedipus Rex*, then, is the sequential arrangement which takes us from Oedipus' promise to free the city from the infection that is plaguing it to his setting out, blinded, into self-imposed exile. A number of events lead, like steppingstones, from that beginning to that ending: Creon's return from the oracle with the news that the infector of the city is the murderer of Laius, who was king before Oedipus; Teiresias' refusal to speak, and then his accusation of Oedipus; the banishment of Creon; Oedipus' conversation with Jocasta, his wife and mother, in which he remembers that it was prophesied that he would kill his father and marry his mother, and in which he remembers, too, how he killed a man under circumstances very like those surrounding the death of Laius; the arrival of the messenger from Corinth with the information that Oedipus' presumed parents, now dead, were not his real parents; the herdsman's confession that, years earlier, he gave the child of Laius and

Jocasta to the messenger from Corinth; Josasta's suicide (off-stage); Oedipus' blinding himself (offstage). The prophecy about Oedipus has been worked out; the prophecy about Laius (that he would die by his son's hand) has been worked out. The cause of the infection has been discovered and removed. The plot has been worked out.

Things occur neatly in *Oedipus Rex*, as in most of the Greek tragedies, each event contributing to the King's discovery and his downfall. At later periods in the history of drama, playwrights began to work several plots into their plays. The word *subplot* is used to describe any sequence of events not directly connected with the main plot. Sometimes a subplot is merely a diversion, a kind of relief—often comic —to distract the audience from the main business of the play. More often, particularly when the playwright has a strong sense of his play as a single well-constructed unit, the subplot has some relation to the main one. In the second act of Jean Giraudoux' *Electra*, after a scene between Electra and Clytemnestra which reveals the extent of jealousy and corruption in their family, there is a lighter scene in which the President of the Council shows that he is jealous of his wife. "You're all pleased, aren't you?" he says. "This little scandal within a great one can't displease you!" The Beggar, who is a kind of commentator and prophet throughout the play, agrees: "No. It's like the squirrel in a big wheel. It gives the right rhythm." This is one of the best descriptions of *subplot* I have ever seen—the little scandal within the larger, the little wheel (made by the running squirrel) within the larger. Although most classical comedies, in which the young man's servant courts the lady's maid while the young man courts the lady, give good examples of a subplot that reflects a main one, the best example in dramatic literature is probably in

King Lear. In that play, while Lear rejects the good Cordelia and is rejected by the two bad daughters in the main plot, Gloucester rejects the good Edgar and is rejected by the bad Edmund in the subplot, a perfect wheel within a wheel.

Plot or subplot, however, we are still at the level of events. My description of *Oedipus Rex* makes it sound like a kind of mystery story in which the murderer is slowly revealed. Such a revelation can be interesting, whether the play is by Sophocles or Agatha Christie, but what happens to Oedipus is much more fascinating than what happens in general. At the opening of the play, he wishes to do the right, the kingly thing—to clean up his city—but his statements reveal his excessive confidence in his own invulnerability, his sense of his own importance (after all, he *did* solve the riddle of the Sphinx). In his arrogance, he forces the unwilling Teiresias to speak and, in the face of the accusation, assumes that he is being hounded not by the truth but by a political plot. Even after the circumstantial evidence begins to weigh him down, he squirms in disbelief, unwilling to be guilty, always demanding one fact more. Jocasta, who sees and is horrified by the truth, goes to her suicide's death before the final evidence is in. When he can no longer struggle, when there is no loophole of interpretation through which he can escape, Oedipus puts out those eyes that have for so long been blind to the truth and accepts the curse that, in his righteous innocence, he called down on Laius' murderer at the beginning of the play: ". . . may he wear out his life/in misery to miserable doom!"

If the plot of *Oedipus Rex* involves the discovery and banishment of Laius' murderer, its action is Oedipus' self-discovery. In most plays, there are two kinds of happenings—those at the level of events and those that go on within the characters. Although *plot* is sometimes used to cover both, it ordinarily describes the external events. *Action* is a word that covers both external and internal happenings; it includes *plot* and goes beyond it. In the chapters that follow, whenever the words *story, plot,* and *action* creep in, you will be able to make some differentiation among them.

Although there is some need to make definitions if we are going to talk about plays, the terminology is much less important than the plays themselves. Whatever the terms one chooses to use, the answer to the question, *What happens?* is still the heart of any play. Action is the first and most important tool of the playwright.

The kind of action depends on the kind of play the dramatist wishes to write, on whether he wants simply to entertain an audience or to mix some kind of enlightenment with his entertainment. Some playwrights concentrate on external events because they want their plays to do no more than excite an audience. The old-fashioned melodrama full of brave swordsmen and ladies in distress is an example. So is the mystery play full of sliding panels and screams of terror. So is the war play with the platoon trapped on a hillside, hoping to outmaneuver a numerically superior enemy. It is difficult, however, for even the most simple-minded playwright to keep from letting his action be internal as well as external. The first thing he knows his swordsman hero has to make a choice between love and honor, his killer turns out to be not crazy but misunderstood and his platoon leader is faced with a moral decision about what one man he dare sacrifice to save the others. The action becomes both external and internal, even though the internal action may be nothing more than the enactment of an obvious kind of cliché. Take as an example all those television westerns in which what happens is not the gunplay itself, but the effect of the gunplay on an adolescent who is about to become a killer because his father did not love him.

External action in its purest form is likely to exist in those plays which are designed only to provoke laughter. *An Italian Straw Hat*, a nineteenth-century French farce by Eugène Labiche and Marc-Michel, provides a good example. In the first act, we discover that Fadinard's horse has eaten an Italian straw hat and that the owner of the hat and her escort have broken into his house and will not leave until the hat is replaced. Since Fadinard is about to get married and since his prospective father-in-law is suspicious, he spends the next four acts hunting a substitute so that he can get the hatless woman out of his house. Fadinard gets involved with a milliner whom he once promised to marry, an aristocratic lady who mistakes him for a famous tenor, and the jealous husband of the woman who lost the hat. The entire wedding party, which follows him around town, mistakes the milliner's shop for the marriage bureau, the aristocrat's home for a restaurant, the husband's home for an inn. There is no point in my attempting to list all the complications that take place before a hat is found and the curtain comes down on a happy ending; from what I have said, it should be clear that the play is simply the piling of one unlikely event on top of another. The play is all plot.

In very few plays, however, is the action all on the surface. Even in broad comedy, internal action usually goes hand in hand with the external. Take Thornton Wilder's *The Matchmaker* as an example. Based on a nineteenth-century farce, Wilder's play is as full of incident as *An Italian Straw Hat*, but all the disguises and the mistaken identities, the accidents and the surprises are devices that contribute to the softening of Horace Vandergelder, the stingy and irascible merchant of Yonkers. The central action of the play is the breaking down of Mr. Vandergelder by Mrs. Levi, the matchmaker of the title, who has decided she wants him for herself.

There is some difficulty about the word *action*. To some literal-minded people, it implies a great deal of busyness, like that in *An Italian Straw Hat*—much running in and out, much opening and closing of doors. Or, on a less frisky level, it suggests swords flashing, pistols going off, bodies falling all over the stage. Although there is a certain amount of fun to be had from watching such activity, it is well to remember that it is genuine action only insofar as it reflects the play's internal action. In the standard western movies about the retired gunslinger who is forced to fight again, the important action comes not when the hero and the villain move slowly toward each other, their gun hands ready, but when the hero buckles on his gunbelt. Just as a small gesture may be more important to a play than a stageful of moiling and toiling, so a line may be more important than a lot of business.

Business is a technical term in the theater; it means the physical activity of the actors on stage. Many people who put on plays load their productions with business on the assumption that audiences are interested in surface activity rather than real action. For this reason, one often sees plays in which the characters wander all over the stage, mixing drinks and lighting cigarettes, going through all kinds of busy work which distracts the audience from what is being said, when the play would be much more exciting if the actors would quit milling around and just sit down and say their lines. I once saw a production of Luigi Pirandello's *Henry IV* which is a good case in point. This play is about a man who may or may not be mad, who has been living for years in a world of make-believe in which he thinks or pretends to think that he is Henry IV, the eleventh-century ruler of the Holy Roman Empire. A plan to bring him back to reality back-fires and, after he stabs one of the planners, he is condemned for the rest of his life to his pretense. The stabbing itself is about the only activity in the play; most of the rest is talk, wonderfully revealing talk which uncovers the complicated relationships among the characters and makes one consider the whole problem of pretense in the supposedly sane world. The opening section of Act I is a scene involving Henry IV's counselors, young men hired to play parts to comfort him in his presumed delusion. They are introducing a new man to the job and, incidentally, introducing the audience to the situation. The director of the production I saw was ap-parently afraid that the audience would not willingly listen to four men carry on a complicated conversation about his-torical periods, so he introduced a great deal of business. The actors ran up and down the stage, dug into boxes full of costumes, pushed each other around in what was supposed to be good-natured horseplay. As a result, the audience had no idea what the men were trying to say and, since their speeches were their part of the play's action, the audience had no idea what the play was about from then on. The play had been sacrificed by a director who had mistaken activity for action.

It is a good idea to watch those people who come away from a play saying "But nothing happens in it," particularly if they add, as a clinching argument, "It was just a lot of talk." There are plays in which talk is activity, not action, but that kind of complaint is ordinarily aimed at those plays in which the action is a little unusual. Samuel Beckett's *Waiting for Godot* is a good example of a play which is sometimes de-scribed as one in which "nothing happens." Two tramps,

Estragon and Vladimir, spend two acts waiting for the arrival of Godot, someone or something who will give direction and meaning to their lives; Godot does not come. Those people who insist that nothing happens in Beckett's play are expecting an arrival, an action that will change the characters and their situation. Since in Beckett's rather black view of the world there can be no change—Estragon and Vladimir are condemned to never having their expectations fulfilled—Godot's not coming is a reflection of the play's real action, which is the waiting. The play is full of business of all kinds—playing around with hats and shoes—and full of apparently pointless talk—jokes and polite conversation—but this activity, unlike the business I described in the bad production of *Henry IV*, is not beside the point. What Estragon and Vladimir do to pass the time while they wait for Godot emphasizes the hopelessness of their waiting. In this case, the surface activity is part of the play's action.

It is necessary in approaching any play not only to ask yourself what happens in it but to be willing to accept that action may take on odd and inactive forms. Judging by most theatrical conventions, Granville Barker's *The Madras House* is one of the most static plays ever written. There is a plot of sorts in which The Madras House, a dressmaking business, is sold to an American businessman, but the sale is only the external reflection of a decision that Philip Madras has come to about the way he wants to live. In a more ordinary play, his reaching that decision might be the internal action, but Philip has made his decision before the curtain goes up on the first act. What Barker does in his play is to use each of the four acts—each in a different setting—as an illustration of the way social and economic pressures affect the way men and women behave toward one another. Although each of the acts has its own action, the play as a whole has no action, at least not in the sense that *Oedipus Rex* or even *Waiting for Godot* has. The action of *The Madras House* is finally demonstration.

One of the most tiresome clichés in any discussion about the theater is the one that uses the phrase "But it's not a play" as a criticism. Ordinary playgoers use it frequently. So, too, do professional critics and professors of drama. What the phrase means of course is that the speaker has a set idea of what a play ought to be and that anything which violates that idea can be dismissed without consideration. It is a lazy man's trick. It is certainly not necessary to like or admire what a particular playwright is trying to do, but it is necessary in approaching any play to understand what is being attempted. That means, first of all, to recognize the action.

4

Who's Got the Action?

For the sake of argument—or at least explanation—it is necessary to separate the elements that go to make up a play, as I have been doing and will continue to do in this book. Still, it is an artificial operation. This is nowhere more apparent than in an attempt to draw a line between action and character. In Chapter 3, when I tried to define the action in *Oedipus Rex*, I used a good part of the space to discuss Oedipus the character. Characters, after all, act out the play's plot; they embody the play's action. Since a character cannot exist without his action, the two things are not really separable. With that assumption written in indelible ink on our foreheads, we can go on to consider character and the mechanics of characterization.

It is one of the clichés of dramatic criticism to condemn characters for lacking *validity* or *depth* or some other respectable quality which, presumably, every character in every play is expected to have. Actually, such terms are only relevant when the playwright is attempting to create characters with a high degree of psychological reality. The kind of character and the method of characterization depend on the kind of play the dramatist is writing. The range is from extremely complicated personalities, realistically presented, to complete abstractions.

In the early 1920s, the students and staff at the Bauhaus in Germany, the school of arts and architecture that Walter Gropius founded, experimented with some theatrical productions in which there was no such thing as character. The actor was disguised in grotesque costumes that hid his human shape; mechanical devices were used to obliterate human sound. The idea, finally, was to reduce man to movement in space, to abstract him completely. In its own way (and less ludicrously) the storyless ballet, such as some of those that George Balanchine choreographs for the New York City Ballet, does the same thing; it converts the action of men into a moving pattern in space. In these theatrical forms, abstraction becomes most complete—the role filled by the performer is something mechanical, not character at all.

In such extreme cases, we are dealing with a form of the theater which is divorced from the play, with a kind of abstraction that is nonhuman rather than generalizing. Drama, however, has its own abstracting tradition. In the Morality plays of the Middle Ages, for instance, the characters were often qualities rather than people—the personified vices and virtues of men or abstractions such as Death and Life. *Everyman*, which is probably the most famous of the Moralities, has many such characters. In that play, Death comes to carry off Everyman. The latter, afraid to make the journey alone, turns to the companions that have been with him through life

—the things around him and the qualities within him—but one by one they fall away. Fellowship, Kindred, Goods, Beauty, Strength, Discretion, Five Wits, finally even Knowledge, who has been most faithful, part from him. At the end, only Good Deeds remains by his side and descends into the grave with him. Like all Morality plays, *Everyman* is designed to teach a lesson. Doctor, who speaks the play's Epilogue, reminds the audience that:

> They all at last do Everyman forsake,
> Alone his Good-Deeds there doth he take.
> But beware, if they be small
> Before God, man hath no help at all.

Although *Everyman* is probably the most dramatic of the Morality plays, and although watching a man being deserted by his friends can be moving and frightening, the play is primarily a message, only incidentally a work of art. For this reason, most of the characters are labels.

The Morality play did not disappear with the end of the Middle Ages, with the sophistication of drama that gave us Shakespeare in Elizabethan times. The teaching play still exists and when it is presented in its simplest, its most direct form, the grand abstractions still walk the stage. During the early 1930s, for instance, when pacifist feeling was very strong in both England and America, there were not only realistic antiwar plays on the commercial stage, but also modern Moralities in the churches and schools. Take as an example a well-meaning English play by Margaret Cropper called *The Pageant of Peace*. In it, War comes to show off his followers (Valour, Renown, Spoils), but is claimed, as father, by another group of abstractions—Hunger, Pain, Sorrow, Want Work, Destruction. After Humility and Love prepare her way, Peace enters and introduces the workers (Hope, Faith, Fortitude, Plenteousness, Joy, Labour, Creative Loveliness) who will help her build the New Jerusalem. Valour deserts War for Peace. Truth is called in to hear both sides and, bringing in Justice, banishes War. "So let the Voice of Truth be heard./Let Peace and Justice be proclaimed among you." Here, the characters are even more obviously walking labels than they are in *Everyman*.

Such abstractions abound in children's plays, particularly in those once-popular quaint offerings—now done infrequently, I hope—in which Happy Childhood was forced to dance with Spring. Not that all abstractions are quite as impersonal-sounding as Happy Childhood and Spring. The New Year's baby who runs across the stage following the bearded Old Year, carrying Time's scythe and hourglass, is such a character. So is Uncle Sam. So, for that matter, are Joseph and Mary as they appear in most amateur Nativity plays, not people at all but animated illustrations out of a Sunday-School paper.

Although pure abstractions are a possibility onstage (it is doubtful that Miss Cropper's characters would ever be more than costumed capital letters), most of them take on personal characteristics in performance. A contemporary production of *Everyman* would almost certainly attempt to differentiate among the abstractions, to make Fellowship, for instance, quite different from Good Deeds. The abstraction, then, is likely to become a type, even when he still bears an abstract name. This tendency is most obvious in advertising where Pain and Dirt are likely to be pictured as monsters who have to be destroyed or gangsters who have to be arrested by the right drug or the strong household cleaner. Mr. Coffee-Nerves, who used to appear in comic-strip advertisements, was simply the old-fashioned villain of melodrama, with the costume and mustache to prove it. These advertising figures—and television cartoons are full of them —are only somewhat foolish examples of abstract characters becoming more than abstractions.

The same device of characterization is apparent in the most sophisticated contemporary playwrights. Death, for instance, appears as a character both in Jean Cocteau's *Orphée* and in Federico García Lorca's *Blood Wedding*. Death, of course, is the abstraction most likely to get into serious plays and he seldom turns up as the conventional figure with the skull face and the black robe. In the plays of both Cocteau and Lorca, Death is a woman. In *Orphée*, she is "a very beautiful young woman in a bright pink evening dress and fur cloak" who must change into a nurse's tunic "of great elegance" when she puts off glamour for pseudo-science in the scene in which she reels in Eurydice's soul. In *Blood Wedding*, she is an old beggar woman who can be commanding, but who is more often whiningly, if threateningly, servile. In neither case is Death a complicated character, one whose subtleties affect and are affected by the action. In both plays, the character's function depends upon the audience's recognizing that she is a familiar type—the glamorous magician in the Cocteau play, the querulous old woman in the Lorca. What we are dealing with here is stereotype, one of the playwright's most convenient tools of characterization.

The word *stereotype* is often used casually as a criticism, as though it were a synonym for *cliché*. In a way it is. A stereotype (or a stock character, to use a more acceptable term) is a character whom the audience knows on sight, whose behavior, whose motivation, whose mannerisms are part of the common fund of information the audience brings to the theater. In effect, what he consists of is the human being seen from only one angle, with the complications and contradictions removed. A stereotype, then, is not untrue; he is rather a partial truth, a one-dimensional truth. More important, he is a familiar truth. He is a kind of cliché, one that the community accepts, and he has a long and respectable family history.

Stock characters were already filling the stage when Menander, the Greek playwright, wrote his comedies in the fourth century B.C. We know the kind of plots and characters he used largely through the Roman imitations, those of Plautus and Terence, written a century or so later. Terence turned out boy-gets-girl comedies which are not too different from our own, except that in Roman times a boy could buy a pretty slave girl if he could afford her. In an ordinary Terence play, a young man spent most of his time trying to outwit his father to get the means to buy the girl, who as likely as not turned out to be a blessing in disguise, someone he was eligible to marry rather than own.

The characters I have mentioned (the angry father, the extravagant young man) and the others in the plays (the tricky servant, the braggart soldier) were stock characters who were recognized by their masks and costumes. Terence used the word *persona* to mean *character*—as we still do when we call the cast list of the play the *dramatis personae*—but the word originally meant mask. In any theater, from one in ancient Greece to the contemporary Berliner Ensemble putting on Bertolt Brecht's *The Caucasian Chalk Circle*, masks are used to represent characters who are types rather than individuals. It is a rare mask that has more than one expression.

Although the mask may represent the stereotype, the

stereotype does not need the mask. In most of the history of Western drama, masks have not been used, but the stereotype, the stock character, still flourishes. Each age has its own stereotypes, some of which it has borrowed from the past and modified to suit its own purposes. The comic doctor is a good example. He goes back at least as far as Renaissance comedy and, at whatever period of history you meet him, you can recognize him by his pomposity, his incompetence, and, most of all, his addiction to the jargon of the trade. You can find him (several of him, in fact) taking advantage of Monsieur Argan in Molière's *The Imaginary Invalid*. You can see him in his most recent disguise in a play like George Axelrod's *The Seven Year Itch*, where he turns up as a psychiatrist eager to get his paperback book through the presses. The persistence of the doctor as a stock comic character probably comes in part from our desire to laugh at a man before whom we are reasonably helpless. Still other characters, not so obviously satirical butts, stay with us. The two comic Irishmen in Sean O'Casey's *Juno and the Paycock* are not only out of the Dublin slums that O'Casey grew up in; they are also out of the warehouse of stock characters which has been open for business since Menander. Captain Boyle, all air and no action, is a seagoing variation on the braggart soldier, and his "butty," Joxer Daly, who spends most of his time agreeing with the Captain while he puts away Boyle's food and drink, is a version of the comic parasite who used to flatter his way to dinner in the Roman comedies.

I do not mean to suggest that either George Axelrod or Sean O'Casey sat down at his desk, saying, as he began to write, "I will now make use of a modern variation on an ancient stock character." These characters—these stereotypes —are part of our own time, as are the dumb blonde, the private eye, the quiet cowboy hero and his comic sidekick, the brat (Dennis the Menace), the Ivy-League account executive, the absent-minded professor, the over-protective mother, the old-maid schoolteacher, the j.d. in the black-leather jacket, and so on. Spend a week of evenings in front of a television set, a month of Friday nights at the movies, a season in the theaters on Broadway, and you can make a list of contemporary stock characters as long as your patience.

For the most part, such characters people our theater. Many playwrights use them consciously, not wanting anything more complicated than the stereotype. Some of them do so because they want to entertain on the simplest level, to spin out a story in which the mechanics of plot absorb an audience, as in a successful spy melodrama. Or to put funny lines into familiar mouths where the laugh is the whole story. Sometimes the playwright wants to educate an audience or to convert it, and his message can be clearer if he uses stereotypes which he knows an audience will accept as representing particular attitudes, classes, races, religions. Whenever the playwright is less interested in character as such than he is in idea, pattern, event, whenever he is less interested in internal action than he is in external, stock characters can serve his purpose. Stereotype, then, is not only a legitimate but also an extremely important device of characterization in the theater.

There are playwrights, however, who want to go beyond stereotype, to approximate as much as possible that complicated creature, the human being. It is in relation to such dramatists—the less successful ones—that we occasionally hear the word *stereotype* used as an attack. A playwright who falls back on the most ordinary kind of psychological clichés, the kind that have been used in soap operas for years, is on safe enough grounds if he wants no more of his play than to draw easy, sentimental tears. If, however, he imagines that his play is doing something more, revealing something about human beings, their relations to one another and to their society, he fails insofar as his characters remain stereotypes. A popular dramatist such as William Inge is a failure on the imaginative level; he is a success as a sentimentalist largely because audiences are moved by the conventions of his plays. In *The Dark at the Top of the Stairs,* for instance, there are two unsuccessful marriages, one oversensitive adolescent who learns a lesson, a member of a minority group whom intolerance drives to suicide, and a little boy who is too dependent on his mother. As Inge presents them, these are stock characters in stock situations, and audiences respond to the stereotype signals they receive. In most of his plays, Inge is quite efficient in the manipulation of such characters, but he fails to the extent that he wants them to be something more than familiar types.

As often as not, those playwrights who do succeed in creating characters of depth and mystery begin with stereotypes. When the audience first sees Hamlet, in the scene in which he wants no part of his mother's marriage to Claudius, he might almost pass for a standard Elizabethan melancholiac, immersed in gloom and loving every moment of it; after all, his mother does suggest that there is something theatrical about Hamlet's excessive mourning, a suggestion that forces him to reply:

> I know not 'seems.'
> 'Tis not alone my inky cloak, good mother,
> Nor customary suits of solemn black,
> Nor windy suspiration of forc'd breath,
> No, nor the fruitful river in the eye,

> Nor the dejected haviour of the visage,
> Together with all forms, moods, shows of grief,
> That can denote me truly.

By the time he gets through his first soliloquy, the one that begins in a manner that any stock melancholiac would love ("O that this too too solid flesh would melt"), the problem about *seems* and true denotation has been set. Hamlet has escaped from his stereotype, and all the scholars, critics, actors, and audiences of three centuries have not been able to force him to wear an identifying label of type. In the same way, Romeo and Juliet are a great deal more than conventional "star-cross'd lovers" and so, too, are their aging colleagues, Antony and Cleopatra. King Lear is far from the choleric old gentleman he sometimes seems to be, and Othello is hardly a typical jealous husband. Yet, these characters are related to the stereotypes I have mentioned. The audience can approach Hamlet through what is immediately familiar in him, perhaps saying *Oh, I know his type,* and then discovering that he is something else, something baffling and not quite definable.

Perhaps the workability of definition is a way of separating the stereotype from the richer character. If a single sentence can adequately describe a character, he is probably a stereotype. If the sentence is true of him but never the whole story, he may have slipped out of the confining single dimension and escaped into multiplicity; he may approach the complications of life. Compare, for instance, the heroines of Henrik Ibsen's *Hedda Gabler* and George Kelly's *Craig's Wife*. Both are cold, destructive women. Harriet Craig manages to drive everyone, including her husband, away from her and her house. Mrs. Craig, who is a social and psychological stereotype, can be summed up in a sentence: she is a woman for whom all possibility of rewarding human relationships has

been sacrificed to a passion for security and material posses-
sions. Except at the very end, when Kelly expects Harriet
Craig to look desolate, to remind us all that the material world
is not enough, everything she does in the play can be explained in terms of her stereotype.

How different Hedda Gabler is. She belittles her husband,
wrecks the trust between Eilert Lövborg and Mrs. Elvsted,
tries to destroy the work they have done together, drives
Eilert to suicide and, at last, commits suicide herself. Her variety does not grow simply out of the fact that the exterior
action in which she is involved is much more complicated than
that of Harriet Craig. Her behavior is more complex. No
single sentence can cover her apparently motiveless cruelty to
her husband's kindly old aunt, her flirtatiousness with Eilert
and Judge Brack, her real or pretended boredom, her moments
of exhilaration, the theatricality of her suicide. Occasionally
an actress plays Hedda as though she were a one-dimensional
monster, a villainess out of nineteenth-century melodrama, and
occasionally a psychologically-oriented critic tries to reduce
her to the stereotype of a specific mental disease, but Hedda,
like Hamlet, refuses to be a jelly jar. No label quite fits her.
You might get near the character with a description such as
this: she is a woman in whom the power of death is greater
than the power of life. But that is so vague that it still gives
Hedda, as a character, plenty of room to maneuver.

Characters, then, range from the simplicity of Good
Deeds to the complexity of Hedda Gabler. Abstraction,
stereotype, individualization—the kind of character depends
on the kind of play as well as on the skill of the playwright. In
reading or seeing any play, it is important not to judge the
characters against some single idea of what a character ought
to be. Henry Aldrich, borrowing a line from T. S. Eliot, might

well say, "I am not Prince Hamlet, nor was meant to be." It is necessary to understand what kind of character the dramatist is trying to create; only then can his success or lack of it be seen.

So far in this chapter, the emphasis has been on kinds of characters. Something needs to be said about the methods of characterization. Whatever degree of complexity a character shows, there are three basic ways for an audience to get to know who and what a character is: (1) by the character's words; (2) by the character's actions; (3) by the reactions, in word and act, of the other characters.

"What messenger art thou?" asks Everyman, and the character replies, "I am Death . . . ." Here, by giving his name, the character has told the audience all that it needs to know about him, although he goes on to spell out his powers. In the medieval drama, the character's own words often identified him directly. Such a device of characterization is still used occasionally, but often the choice of words tells us as much as the direct statement. In a scene on a bus in *It Happened One Night*, one of Frank Capra's movie comedies, a traveling salesman sits down next to the heroine and introduces himself: "My name's Shapely, and that's the way I like them." From this line alone we know not only who he is and what he is after, but that he has a pat approach, that he imagines himself a wit, and that his brashness is so obvious that he is not likely to get anywhere with the heroine, who is more sophisticated than he.

In Christopher Fry's *The Lady's Not for Burning*, the heroine, having just escaped from a mob that wants to burn her as a witch, tells the mayor and his family, from whom she is seeking sanctuary, "I am Jennet Jourdemayne/And I believe in the human mind." In this instance, the self-identification has

become a great deal more complicated than "I am Death
. . . ." Jennet does know her name, but the rest of the statement cannot be taken at face value. Her line is, first of all, a
plea that those around her will protect her, a hopeful assumption that so civilized-looking a household could not believe in
witches as do her would-be burners, "Those old credulous
children in the street." Beyond that, the line is, or so Jennet
thinks, a statement of fact. She is professedly a believer in the
human mind, by which she means a rationalist, one who is
concerned only with, as she later says, "What I touch, what
I see, what I know; the essential fact." One of the things that
happens in the play is that Jennet comes to accept a world of
mystery and surprise, is convinced by Thomas Mendip that
the essential facts are not seeable or touchable. As the change
in her takes place, we can see how the playwright used the
character's self-identification as a means to present her character. We see Jennet as a positive young woman who means
what she says, but who has not yet learned that what she says
has a larger meaning than she intends; she does not yet understand that the human mind offers, as one of Christopher Marlowe's characters put it, "Infinite riches in a little room."

In the examples given in the two preceding paragraphs,
the characters are attempting to explain themselves, but our
understanding of characters can hardly depend on self-analy-
sis. Whatever words a character speaks onstage help identify
him. The problem for the audience, as my reading of Jennet
Jourdemayne's line indicates, is to decide what the words
mean, to the playwright and to the character. Imagine a scene,
on- or offstage, in which a boy is offered a piece of chocolate
cake and refuses, saying, "No thank you." The line tells us
something about the boy, but what? He does not like chocolate cake? He has tasted the offerer's cake before and does

not like it? He has been brought up to be polite by a mother who imagines that politeness can only be displayed by refusal? He is simply not hungry? He has a mouthful of chewing gum and no place to put it? These are only a few of the possibilities. As the example indicates, words tell us something, but only when we are able to consider them in a context and have a chance to judge that context against others. Lines onstage, like lines offstage, break down into three basic categories: (1) presumed truths which are true; (2) presumed truths which are false because the speaker lacks information or self-knowledge; (3) conscious lies, detected or undetected. There are many complications implicit in these three categories, some of which we will examine in detail in Chapter 5, on language. For now, it is enough to recognize that the words a character speaks are part of the dramatist's means to his characterization, but that such a recognition does not demand that we believe everything the character says.

As with words, so with acts. What a character does helps define him. Take a ludicrous example. When the curtain goes up on Jean Anouilh's *Thieves' Carnival*, Eva and Hector are discovered in a passionate embrace. When the kiss ends, they exchange a few words which might be those of people in love, but then comes the business of the hand. "I want to inhale the perfume of your hand!" pleads Hector. As he bends low over the hand, he whips out a jeweler's glass and examines her rings. The audience recognizes the thief behind the lover, but the scene also reveals something important about Eva. As she offers her hand to Hector, she turns and watches Lord Edgard, an old family friend, who is sitting nearby reading a paper. Since the play is a farce, one might say that her turning away is simply a playwright's device which lets him make his joke with Hector and the jeweler's glass. Since Eva indicates that she does not want to be discovered, she may have good reason to keep a wary eye on Lord Edgard. The gesture is a device, of course, and it can be explained in terms of plot, but it is much more important as an indication of the basic indifference of Eva which will become increasingly obvious as the play goes on.

The business with the jeweler's glass is a very special case, of course, an elaborate set-up in which the playwright can score a comic point as well as identify one of his characters. For the most part, it is the ordinary things that a character does onstage that tell an audience about him—the way he opens doors, the attentions he pays to another character, the way he holds his fork (or his sword), the way he starts whenever a bell rings. Othello's strangling of Desdemona is not the kind of onstage act which can tell us much about him; if we have not begun to know Othello by then, we never will know him. The strangling is part of the play's over-all action and not a device of characterization.

In considering what a character does onstage, the audience must recognize that his acts, like his words, have to be interpreted. An act can be a lie as easily as a word can. A handshake or a kiss offered as a conventional cover to mask one's dislike of another person is such a lying act. In another context, that handshake or kiss may be an unconscious lie, a conventional gesture by a man who does not yet recognize his feelings for the person whose hand he shakes, whose cheek he kisses. I do not want to pile up examples here, since the playwright's use of gesture will be examined in greater detail in a later chapter. Here it is enough to accept that the playwright can use what a character does to indicate what he is like. Still, the meaning of the character's acts must be as carefully considered as the meaning of his words, particularly, as with Hector in *Thieves' Carnival,* when the words and the acts contradict one another.

An audience finally comes to understand a character by considering what he says and what he does alongside the way other characters react to him. Here too, we are faced with the problem of interpretation, for the reactions, whether they are words or acts, may be genuine or feigned, may be as true or false as the lines and acts considered in the paragraphs above. For, of course, while one character describes another he is helping to characterize not only the person described but himself.

At the simplest level, we have description. Jean Anouilh's *Antigone* opens with all the characters on stage, sitting or standing in poses which we will come to recognize as characteristic of them. The playwright uses a chorus—one man, as in Shakespeare's *Henry V*—to get things under way; he steps forward and introduces each of the characters, giving a brief description of what he or she is like. Since Chorus presumably is speaking for the playwright, since he has nothing to hide as a character, we can accept what he says as true. To use a chorus, a narrator, a commentator, someone outside the action who can talk about it, is an ancient device that is increasingly popular in the contemporary theater, but it can only be used in plays in which the audience is not asked to pretend that the stage illusion is real. At the turn of the century, when realistic theater was at its strongest, dramatists sometimes put into their plays a character, called the *raissoneur,* who had no vital part to play in the action but who always seemed to be around; he could be used as Anouilh uses Chorus.

Even when such artificial means are not possible, the playwright often puts into the mouths of some of his characters information that will help explain others. If one character says of another, "He's an engineer," or "He's from Des Moines," or "He's a Catholic," or "I knew his mother, she spoiled him," the lines may well be simply informational. In most cases, when we hear such a line in a play, we can accept it as true unless there is something about the speaker or the person spoken to which calls the descriptive phrase in doubt. Sometimes the description is true enough, but the playwright uses the speech to help with more than one characterization. Near the beginning of *The Sea Gull*, Chekhov sets up a scene in which Treplev describes his mother in great and angry detail. Since he is speaking to his uncle, who knows Arkadina as well as the young man does, Treplev's speech can hardly be taken as a simple explanation. Much of what he says about Arkadina is information the audience can use, but the way he says it tells us more about him than it does about her.

Nonverbal reactions are as useful as spoken lines in indicating what a character is like. One example should be enough to illustrate what I mean. Maxwell Anderson wants us to know that the heroine of his *Mary of Scotland* is a charming woman. We first meet her on the pier at Leith, as she arrives in Scotland to rule as queen. There to meet her is John Knox, who has come to denounce her. Already characterized as an angry and implacable man, John Knox has only to soften a little, to kiss her hand (still insisting that he disapproves of her), for us to see that the girl has charm. The reaction, of course, also tells us something about John Knox. Whenever one character reacts to another—showing boredom, joy, fear, admiration, astonishment, common courtesy—the audience learns something about both of them.

To understand what is going on in a play, as I suggested

at the beginning of this chapter, one must know the characters. Whether they are abstractions or stock figures or attempts at psychological validity, we can only come to know them by watching and listening. In the next chapter, I want to consider the kinds of language we can expect to hear.

5

The Language of Words

The kind of language that a playwright uses depends on the playwright himself—the kind of play he wants to write, the characters he creates, the century he writes in. George Bernard Shaw once said that if he had lived in Elizabethan times he would have taken to blank verse and given Shakespeare a run for his money. Although Shaw may have made the statement, as he made so many others, in order to hear the Shakespeare lovers scream, it does carry an important implication about the use of stage language. Every period has its own conventions. Still, the dominant stage language does not preclude the use of others. Thus, Elizabethan drama is primarily a poetic one, even though most of the plays of the period have extensive prose passages—usually in the comic scenes. Some of Shakespeare's prose scenes—for instance, the one in *Macbeth* in which the drunken porter takes his time answering the knocking at the gate—are as famous as the verse soliloquies one had to learn in high school: "To-morrow, and to-morrow, and to-mor-row/Creeps in this petty pace . . . ." Similarly, our own theater is primarily a prose one and has been since the middle of the nineteenth century when a few strong-minded play-wrights, of whom Henrik Ibsen is the most important, proved that serious plays need not be written in verse. This does not mean, of course, that there are not many contemporary play-wrights who do write in verse, or try to. Even Arthur Miller, who is celebrated for his command of American colloquial speech, used a not-very-successful free verse for some of the lawyer's speeches in the first version of *A View from the Bridge*. A playwright's language is likely to represent a com-promise between the conventions of the stage he writes for and his willingness to violate those conventions.

There is no one kind of language suitable for the stage. I have heard a man come away from a verse drama complain-ing because, as he put it, "People don't talk poetry." I have seen the same man come away from a musical comedy per-fectly happy, not at all bothered by the fact that people do not sing their sentiments. His initial complaint may have meant any number of things: that he did not like that partic-ular play, that he does not like verse, that he is unwilling to listen to it. Whatever was really bothering him, his explicit complaint has no validity. People onstage do sometimes speak poetry, just as they sometimes sing their hearts out. Every kind of stage language is a convention, and it is the audience's job to accept the convention he is watching. I do not mean that he has to find the poetry or the prose good; quality is another problem altogether. I mean simply that a play in verse should not be attacked for being unrealistic, and a play writ-ten in prose idiom should not be accused of being unpoetic.

There is really only one inescapable requirement for language for a play—that it be speakable. At a conference on drama, an eminent playwright once said that he did not think like a literary man, that words did not come to him as patterns on the page, but as speeches from the mouth of some character or other. This is the one important distinction between the playwright and another kind of writer: he does not see a line in his mind's eye, he hears it in his mind's ear. There is, of course, the question of what is or is not speakable. Lazy audiences and lazy actors sometimes use the criterion of speakability as an excuse for their own shortcomings. An audience who is unwilling to pay attention, or an actor who imagines that all characters, in and out of plays, speak exactly as he does, sometimes brands as unspeakable lines that are difficult, subtle, intricate. If the lazy had their way, all stage language would become infantile. The best playwrights, the demanding playwrights—Shakespeare and Shaw, to stick with the Englishmen—do not write unspeakable lines, but they often write complicated ones which demand articulation from the actors and attention from the audience.

Scattered through the paragraphs above are references to particular kinds of stage language, introduced in a somewhat haphazard way. To be a little more orderly, the language of the stage can be divided into four general categories: (1) colloquial prose; (2) literary prose; (3) verse; and (4) language to accompany music.

The first of these, colloquial prose, is the end product of the desire to make what happens on stage as real as possible —not psychologically real, or spiritually real necessarily, but real to the eye and the ear. The playwright who works in this idiomatic way tries to make his characters speak as nearly as possible like their counterparts in real life. As a result, slang, common grammatical errors, special regional usages, clichés of all kinds get into the lines. The playwright's job is not to write beautiful lines, but characteristic ones; most of all, he tries to avoid expressions or sentence structure which his characters would be unlikely to use. Listen to Ruth Younger in Lorraine Hansberry's *A Raisin in the Sun* complaining to her mother-in-law: "No—he don't half try at all 'cause he knows you going to come along behind him and fix everything. That's just how come he don't know how to do nothing right now—you done spoiled that boy so." Ruth is a working-class Negro woman, living in a Chicago slum, and Miss Hansberry wants her speech to reflect both her education and her environment. *Done spoiled*, for instance, is a grammatical error that is probably more rural than urban (at least onstage, that verb form is often in the mouth of a farmer), a fact which seems to indicate that the speech in a Negro slum still reflects the Southern origin of many of its inhabitants even though the particular speaker may have been born in Chicago. In contrast to Ruth and to Mama, Beneatha, Ruth's sister-in-law, who is going to college, speaks lines which are free of such obvious grammatical errors but are full of slang.

Listen to Mrs. Fusari pestering the hero of Paddy Chayefsky's television play *Marty:* "My son Frank, he was married when he was nineteen years old. Watsa matter with you?" The quotation is a little short to catch the rhythm of the Bronx speech which is characteristic of Chayefsky's television plays, but the *my son*, the double subject ("Frank, he"), the slurred *watsa* are all indications of the background of the play —an urban neighborhood in which elements of foreign speech are still strong and in which there is a dominating family structure.

On stage, there is little problem with colloquial speech so long as the actor can achieve and hold on to the correct accent.

On the page, however, such speech presents difficulties. The playwright uses spelling devices which would be all right if they were simply hints to the actor, but which present contradictions to the reader. Take Chayefsky's *watsa matter* as an example. Obviously a person who says *watsa* is going to say *matta* or *mattah*. In the same way, Miss Hansberry's Ruth is not likely to say *going to* but *gonna* and the *g*'s will probably disappear from all her *ing* words. A playwright who attempts to do more than indicate the way a line should be read is likely to fall into one of two traps. He may write barely recognizably lines, as George Bernard Shaw did when he attempted to reproduce Bill Walker's speech in *Major Barbara:* "But thets aw rawt, you knaow. Nathink pasnl. Naow mellice. Sao long, Judy." He may write lines that sound like parodies of actual speech as Eugene O'Neill did in *The Iceman Cometh* where Margie says "Jees, Poil, it's de Morgue wid all de stiffs on deck," and Wetjoen, who is supposed to be a Boer from South Africa, says, "Dey vill be so glad I haf come home at last."

The chief drawback of the use of colloquial language has nothing to do with the difficulties of presenting it on the page. Once we accept that what we are reading is the suggestion of a particular dialect or accent, and not an accurate transcription of it, our imaginations can do the rest. The weakness in a playwright's dependence on colloquial speech is that it is too often used to present almost inarticulate people. In an attempt to avoid literary prose, a playwright can become so intent on not violating his characters verbally that he does away with all vividness. That, of course, is not necessary. It is true that much of ordinary speech is a matter of grunts, wheezes, puffs, and hand signals, which are ways of communicating between people who know one another fairly well.

Despite this, ordinary speech, in whatever country, has its own color and rhythm. Metaphor, for instance, is not simply a poetic device; it is a common way of speaking. In *A Raisin in the Sun*, Ruth calls the apartment they live in a "rat trap," a phrase which is both a metaphor and a cliché, but which is particularly appropriate to the situation; the Youngers want desperately to get out of the slum where they have been trapped too long by color and by poverty. The words that make up colloquial speech can, then, contribute not only to a play's milieu, but to its action and its theme.

Colloquial speech can also be attractive in its own right. The early plays of Clifford Odets provide many examples. In *Awake and Sing!* which takes place in the Bronx twenty years before Chayefsky's *Marty*, Bessie Berger comments on her father's ability to talk and the uselessness of that talk in the middle of a depression: "He should try to buy a two-cent pickle in the Burland Market without money." Bessie's line is not only colloquial; it is as neat and economical as a good line of poetry, making its point with a projected image, a penniless Jacob trying to and failing to trade his book-learned socialism for a dill pickle. If Odets seems an unlikely playwright to choose to indicate the possible richness of colloquial speech, perhaps we should consider John Millington Synge, who is usually praised by critics for his poetic language. In a short "Preface" to *The Playboy of the Western World*, Synge says, "I have used one or two words only that I have not heard among the country people of Ireland." He goes on to make a special case for the idiom of rural Ireland: "In countries where the imagination of the people, and the language they use, is rich and living, it is possible for a writer to be rich and copious in his words, and at the same time to give the reality, which is the root of all poetry, in a comprehensive and natural form."

Listen to Synge's Christy Mahon speaking of Pegeen Mike, when he thinks he is about to lose her:

> for there's torment in the splendor of her like, and she's a girl any moon of midnight would take pride to meet, facing southwards on the heaths of Keel. But what did I want crawling forward to scorch my understanding at her flaming brow?

With Synge, and even with Odets, colloquial speech is not simply reproduced; it takes on artistic form. For this reason, it might be considered a kind of literary prose, but it is not what I mean by that phrase as I used it a few pages back. Perhaps another quotation from *Major Barbara* will indicate what I do mean more clearly than an abstract statement can. Even though Shaw does attempt sometimes, as with Bill Walker above, to indicate a particular accent, his characters do not speak as ordinary men do. Their lines are carefully constructed prose passages. Here is Andrew Undershaft explaining the "true faith of an Armourer:"

> To give arms to all men who offer an honest price for them, without respect of persons or principles: to aristocrat and republican, to Nihilist and Tsar, to Capitalist and Socialist, to Protestant and Catholic, to burglar and policeman, to black man, white man and yellow man, to all sorts and conditions, all nationalities, all faiths, all follies, all causes and all crimes.

This is not ordinary conversation. This is a speech to be delivered from the stage, as artificial in its way as any soliloquy in Shakespeare. We can imagine its being made from a public platform perhaps, but not in a simple exchange between one man and another. The piling on of example—beginning with the string of compounds ("aristocrat and republican," "Nihilist and Tsar"), passing on to a triple ("black man, white man and yellow man"), building to a stack of *alls*—is a rhetorical device used by a man who recognizes that sentences can be manipulated for effect. Shaw, who was an inveterate public speaker, willing, at least in his younger days, to talk almost anywhere on almost any subject, used all the tricks he learned on the platform to give the speeches in his plays form, even elegance. The artificiality that I have been describing does not mean that the speeches Shaw wrote were inappropriate for the characters who spoke them. They were not. The use of literary prose, like the use of verse, simply colors the surface presentation of a character.

The accurate reproduction of colloquial speech is no guarantee that a character is believably real or a revelation to the audience or even interesting. The judge in Enid Bagnold's *The Chalk Garden* quotes the words that a convicted murderer spoke just before he sentenced her: "What I have been listening to in court is not my life. It is the shape and shadow of my life. With the accidents of truth taken out of it." Before these lines are spoken, we have watched Miss Madrigal (the murderer, now pardoned) for almost two acts, have seen her concern with truth and the pretenses that disguise it; so the line when it comes is perfectly hers, although it is spoken by another mouth. Try rewriting the line colloquially. "All this stuff I've heard in court is not true. It's true, but it's not really true." Something like that, I suppose. In reality, a young woman being sentenced, even an articulate one, might more likely speak my revision than the line Miss Bagnold wrote, but on stage, particularly for Miss Madrigal, Miss Bagnold's line is the accurate one. The test of a line in a play is never its relation to ordinary speech, but its relation to the other lines in the play and its appropriateness to the speaker. *The Chalk Garden* is a prose play, but not a colloquial one.

By using as my examples George Bernard Shaw, the best writer of prose ever to work for the English stage, and Enid Bagnold, who has a fine way with words, I have probably given the wrong impression about the use of literary prose on the stage. A great many quite ordinary plays written by not very eloquent playwrights are in literary prose, but there seems little point in multiplying examples. It is enough, perhaps, to re-emphasize that the basic language of the contemporary stage is prose, whether colloquial or literary (and sometimes the line between them almost disappears), and that the dominance of prose is a relatively new thing. Verse has been the traditional language of the theater.

The basic verse, for the English stage at least, is unrhymed iambic pentameter, the blank verse that Shakespeare used. Pentameter is a line which has five feet in it—a foot being a unit into which we divide a poetic line to speak it—and an iamb is a foot with two beats, the first unstressed, the second stressed. A line of Shakespeare's should make the versification clear. I opened my Shakespeare at random and happened to hit the last page of *Henry V*, where the first line of Chorus' Epilogue will suit our purposes: "Thus far with rough and all-unable pen . . . ."

Thŭs fár / wĭth roúgh / ănd aĺl- / ŭn á / blĕ pén

This is a line of iambic pentameter with the feet marked off by diagonals (/) and the stressed ( ) and unstressed ( ) beats clearly indicated. The Elizabethan dramatists presumably hit on this particular meter because it is so natural to English-speaking people. We use the rhythm ordinarily. Take the line I have just written:

We use / the rhy / thm or / di nar / i ly

It, too, is iambic pentameter.

Although iambic pentameter is his basic line, Shakespeare does not use it consistently. As often as not, an extra syllable creeps in, the stresses change within a line, the number of feet varies. Let us go on with Chorus' speech: "Thus far with rough and all-unable pen/Our bending author hath pursu'd the story . . . ."

Our bend / ing au / thor hath / pur su'd / the sto ry

This is a simple variation on the standard line, an expected one. Often when the line ends in a two-syllable word, the last foot has an extra unstressed beat. Take another line at random, one from the Queen's last speech: "As man and wife, being two, are one in love . . . ."

As man / and wife / be ing two / are one / in love

Here, the middle foot is not an iamb, but an anapest, two un-stressed syllables followed by a stressed one. Pick up any of Shakespeare's plays and, on any page, you will find a great many lines which are not iambic pentameter. There is no point in making a longer catalogue here. It is enough to recognize that iambic pentameter gives Shakespeare's verse its basic beat, a key to the way both the regular and the irregular lines are to be spoken and heard.

The verse I have been describing was used not only by Shakespeare and his contemporaries but has been copied by most English playwriting poets ever since. There was a time in the late seventeenth century when English playwrights, copying the French tragedians Racine and Corneille, used rhymed verse to write their tragedies. Here is Boabdelin, at the opening of John Dryden's *The Conquest of Granada:*

> Thus, in the triumphs of soft peace, I reign;
> And, from my walls, defy the powers of Spain;
> With pomp and sports my love I celebrate,
> While they keep distance, and attend my state.

Even though he writes in rhymed couplets, Dryden was English enough to hold on to the pentameter line instead of trying to write the longer French line; in his most famous play, *All for Love*, he went back to blank verse.

Rhyme has never really become much of a force in the writing of dramatic verse in English. It is used, for the most part, only for incidental effect—often no more than a decoration closing out a scene. For instance, the last scene of *Henry V* ends on the King's: "Then shall I swear to Kate, and you to me,/And may our oaths well kept and prosp'rous be!" The effect of the rhymed couplet here, after the blank verse preceding it, is to provide a neat cutting-off, an ending that sounds like an ending. Although I never indicated it in my discussion above, the Epilogue is also in rhyme. It begins

> Thus far, with rough and all-unable pen,
> Our bending author hath pursu'd the story,
> In little room confining mighty men,
> Mangling by starts the full course of their glory.

The rhyme here works to give the Chorus' speech a formality that divides it from the lines in the play itself; the speech is a summing-up and is separate from the action of the play. In contemporary verse plays, too, rhyme is seldom used except for special effects, often comic ones, as in *The Dog beneath the Skin*, by W. H. Auden and Christopher Isherwood, where the silly lovers (sitting in a tree) talk like this:

> Little white dove, it's you that I love,
> Fairer than hollyhocks far!
> How nice and how neat

> Are your dear little feet!
> You make my heart beat!
> How terribly sweet, how terribly sweet,
> How terribly sweet you are!

In discussing verse as stage language, I have pretty much restricted myself to talking about meter and rhyme. One other point should probably be made to indicate a division among writers of stage verse. Two contemporary dramatic poets, T. S. Eliot and Christopher Fry, can serve as examples. In his early plays, Eliot experimented in many ways, varying meter, adding rhyme, multiplying metaphor, but by the time he got around to writing *The Cocktail Party* in 1949, he had decided that verse should be as close to prose as possible. It should simply supply an underlying rhythm which could hold the actors and the audience, preparing them for the important scenes in which, presumably, the verse would add an intensity that prose could not. Take a speech at random, one that Edward makes to Peter in the first act:

> There's no memory you can wrap in camphor
> But the moths will get in. So you want to see Celia.
> I don't know why I should be taking all this trouble
> To protect you from the fool you are.
> What do you want me to do?

The lines seem to have no set meter; they would probably be read the same way if they were written as prose. More important, in contrast to Fry's lines, they are simple, spare. It is true that there is a metaphor which compares memory to something locked in a cedar chest, but it is a functional metaphor, a way of telling Peter that nothing remains static, unchanged. Contrast such lines with those that Alizon speaks in *The Lady's Not for Burning* when she first enters:

Coming in from the light, I am all out at the eyes.
Such white doves were paddling in the sunshine
And the trees were as bright as a shower of broken glass.
Out there, in the sparkling air, the sun and the rain
Clash together like the cymbals clashing
When David did his dance. I've an April blindness.
You're hidden in a cloud of crimson Catherine-wheels.

The passage is typical of Fry. Alizon, one of the least eloquent of his characters, takes the long way around to say that moving from the bright sun light into the darker room has momentarily blinded her. The contrast here is between verse that is functional only and verse that is decorative, that takes pleasure in its own glittering surface. Not that Fry's glitter is not functional, too, since it gives the whole play a feeling of richness, invention, surprise, which is part of the concept of life that makes Thomas Mendip, the hero who wants to be hanged, decide to live. This contrast, of course, is not one that is limited to the writers of verse; prose, too, may be spare or lush, functional or decorative. The thing to watch for, whether the language is verse or prose, is how well it works within the play as a whole.

It is possible that my initial division of stage language should have had two rather than four categories. As colloquial and literary prose are inescapably connected, so words meant to be sung are likely to be verse. The fourth category is, of course, the most artificial of all the kinds of stage language. It is, however, no more of a convention than the speaking of prose or verse. Once the convention is accepted, the words to be sung can be treated like any other stage words—with one important exception: the music. The meaning of spoken words can change, of course, according to the way the actor speaks them. He can say "You look lovely" in a tone of voice that means "You look ghastly." Music does much the same thing. It can intensify the meaning of the words, contradict them, mock them. Take an outrageous example from the Leonard Bernstein musical, *Candide*. Candide, meeting Cunegonde after their forceful separation, sings: "Dearest how can this be so?/You were dead, you know./You were shot and bayoneted, too." Cunegonde comes in with "That is very true./Ah, but love will find a way."* The words are harsh; the tune is a sweet and sentimental lover's duet. The result is a satirical comment on the cliché about love's finding a way. The language of the musical stage is not that much different from other kinds of stage language. The important thing to remember is that the language in the former case is a combination of music and words.

Language in a play, whether it is prose or verse, works pretty much as language does offstage. One of its jobs is to supply information to the audience. The playwright can do this most easily by providing his play with a narrator or a commentator who tells the audience exactly what it needs to know; the role of Chorus from Jean Anouilh's *Antigone*, which I described in the last chapter, is a good example of such a device. When he does not want to make use of a character outside the action, the playwright must contrive other ways of passing on the necessary information. The soliloquy and the aside are traditional ways of doing that. The soliloquy is a speech, such as Hamlet's "O, what a rogue and peasant slave am I," in which the character, talking to himself, goes through a self-examination which the audiences over-

* From "You Were Dead, You Know," by John Latouche and Richard Wilbur, from *Candide*, by Lillian Hellman and Leonard Bernstein. Copyright 1957 by John Latouche and Richard Wilbur; reprinted by permission of Random House Publishers.

hears. The aside is a remark aimed directly at the audience, an interruption of and a comment on the conventional dialogue. The aside was popular well through the nineteenth century, but to see it at its busiest one should read a Restoration comedy, such as William Wycherley's *The Country Wife,* where it is in continual use. A single instance: Pinchwife, the jealous husband who has been keeping his wife hidden from the gallants, is upset when he learns that he was seen at the theater with "a pretty country-wench"; he says, aside, for the benefit of the audience: "How the devil! did he see my wife then?"

With the coming of realistic theater, the playwright had to find a new means to provide exposition, had to let characters explain things to one another—sometimes, unfortunately, things that all of them would be likely to know. The stage servant, the butler who has to be told what is going on by the housekeeper, became a standard device; he often has no function as a character, but is simply a mechanism for getting things explained to the audience. A favorite example of mine, perhaps because it is an early one, is from Robert Browning's *A Blot in the 'Scutcheon.* Here the 2nd Retainer says to the warrener:

> Now, Gerard, out with it!
> What makes you sullen, this of all the days
> I' the year? To-day that young rich bountiful
> Handsome Earl Mertoun, whom alone they match
> With our Lord Tresham through the country-side,
> Is coming here in utmost bravery
> To ask our master's sister's hand?

If the audience had not needed to know the immediate situation and the background of the leading characters, the questioner would have stopped with *year.*

In time, playwrights became adept at giving information

without putting unlikely speeches in the mouths of characters. The opening of George Bernard Shaw's *Getting Married* is as good an example as any. The first line is spoken by a woman sitting reading by the fire, to a man in evening dress, counting napkins. She says, "Do you never feel nervous on these occasions, Collins?" and he answers, "Lord bless you, no, maam. It would be a joke, after marrying five of your daughters, if I was to get nervous over marrying the last of them." From the first exchange we know that he is working for her, that his name is Collins and that the occasion is a wedding, but there is no strain in imparting the information. Within a few more sentences we learn, just as simply, that she is the wife of an Anglican Bishop and then, as we go on through the play, we pick up, casually, the information that will help us identify the other characters and react to them.

Stage language is not as simple as this discussion of exposition might indicate. I have been talking about lines which are designed to communicate something, in which the character is presumably speaking the truth. There's the problem. Since language in a play belongs not only to the playwright but to the character who speaks it, we must always consider the words in a play in the context of situation. A character may deliberately lie to achieve his purpose. Murder mysteries could not exist without such lying. Language onstage then—like language in life—is not only a way of communicating, but a way of not communicating. Many of the lines in plays are simply practical ones and we can take them as truths ("I'm home, dear") or as unimportant lies ("That's a pretty hat you're wearing"). Even such apparently obvious lines take on special implications when we consider who the speaker is and to whom he is talking. Imagine a situation in which "I'm home, dear" is not a greeting but the establishment of an alibi. Or one in which "That's a pretty hat . . ." is not a polite social lie, but the first move in a character's plan to ingratiate himself with someone he plans to cheat or seduce or murder.

Purposeful truth and deliberate lying are direct uses of language. The best playwrights are those who use words obliquely, who let the character speak without being aware of what he is saying. Listen to Treplev in *The Sea Gull*:

> TREPLEV, *pulling petals from a flower:* She loves me . . . she loves me not . . . she loves me . . . she loves me not . . . loves me . . . loves me not. *Laughing.* See, my mother doesn't love me. But, then, why should she? She wants to live, have love affairs, and wear pretty clothes; and here I am—twenty-five —always reminding her that she's getting older. When I'm not around, she's thirty-two; when I am, she's forty-three . . . and she hates me for it. And she knows that I despise the theatre! She *loves* the theatre, and thinks she's serving humanity! But in my opinion our theatre's in a rut. It's nothing but clichés and shopworn conventions. When the curtain opens on those three-walled "living rooms," and I see those famous and talented actors, those high priests of that sacred art, parade about in their costumes in front of the footlights showing the way people eat, drink, make love, and walk about; when I hear them try to squeeze a moral out of commonplace phrases and meaningless events—some cliché that everyone knows and is suitable for home consumption; when they give me a thousand variations of the same old thing over and over again . . . I have to leave! I want to run away as Maupassant ran away from the Eiffel Tower because its vulgarity was destroying him.*

In Chapter 2, I discussed *The Sea Gull* briefly, talked about Treplev's desire to impress his mother through his writing. In this speech he gives away a great deal more of himself than

---

* From "The Sea Gull," *Six Plays of Chekhov*, Rinehart Editions, trans. Robert W. Corrigan, by permission of Holt, Rinehart & Winston.

he intends. It opens with a direct discussion of his mother and her presumed rejection of him, then passes on to a discussion of the esthetics of the popular theater of his time. There is no reason to suppose that Treplev is not sincere in his denunciation of that theater, but it is useless to confuse sincerity with motivation. Here, we see him reacting to his mother's *love* for the theater, which he sees as a rival. It is the world of the theater, in which she functions as a center of attraction, that makes her prefer not to be a mother saddled with a grown son. Treplev then lists all that is wrong with Arkadina's kind of theater (and these are genuine limitations of the nineteenth-century theater), as though he were recording the blemishes of a rival. The speech ends with his desire to run away from that theater, the scene of his defeat in the struggle for his mother's love. Being Treplev, he explains his longed-for escape in esthetic terms; being a Russian intellectual at the turn of the century, hence an admirer of French literature, he goes to Maupassant for his example. Chekhov wants us to recognize that Treplev is a complicated character, an egotistical young man eaten by a number of related grievances. There is, quite obviously, an important relationship between his unhappiness about his mother and his concern as a young writer, but he must never recognize that; his words do the revealing against his will.

What a character says, then, may be colored by what he fails to know about himself. Or refuses to know, because, in some cases, the truth may be unattractive and the character chooses not to recognize it. For that reason, a character's speech, whatever it is about, may be a way of lying to himself. This may even be the case with the soliloquies in Shakespeare, in which, as I suggested above, the character is presumably giving an honest self-examination. It is at least arguable that

Hamlet's soliloquies, in which he chides himself for not acting to revenge his father, are not attempts to face his own hesitancy, but devices which let him substitute rumination for action.

Any speech in a play, then, may have two uses. The character may use it for some purpose within a scene while the playwright uses it to comment on that scene—to tell us something about the speaker perhaps. Irony depends on this double nature of the dramatic line. Irony occurs when a line reveals something more than what is literally said, when the audience is able to see that something a character says is true in a way that the character could not know. Take a comic example. The hero of Oscar Wilde's *The Importance of Being Earnest*, whom the audience knows as John Worthing, calls himself Ernest to please a young lady who likes the name; he learns, at the end of the play, that his real name is Ernest. In retrospect, his insistence on the presumably false name becomes ironical. Since the audience discovers the true name at the same time the hero does, the irony of the lines is not apparent when they are spoken. In a play in which the audience has knowledge ahead of the hero, the playwright can use apparently innocent lines to achieve irony. In *Oedipus Rex*, where the irony is certainly not comic, the audience knows that Oedipus is guilty from the beginning, and as a result all of his lines have two meanings—one for his ignorance, one for our knowledge.

The literary devices that a playwright makes use of—metaphor and symbol, for instance—are subject to the same ambiguity all stage speeches are. A metaphor may belong to the playwright, the character, or both at once. I suggested that Ruth's use of "rat trap" in *A Raisin in the Sun* was her own, that is, a colloquial usage that might well come from such a character's mouth, and, at the same time, Miss Hansberry's comment on the family's desperate need to move. Take another example, the opening speech from Tennessee Williams' *The Glass Menagerie*. Tom, who is both character and narrator, describes the background of the play:

> the huge middle class of America was matriculating in a school for the blind. Their eyes had failed them, or they had failed their eyes, and so they were having their fingers pressed forcibly down on the fiery Braille alphabet of a dissolving economy.

That is, it was the 1930s and the Depression was on. Tom is a would-be poet, one who might make a metaphor so elaborate that it becomes finally a little foolish, but Tom is also rather like the author in many details of his life and it is possible that the narrator speaks for the author, that Williams admires the metaphor. In *A Streetcar Named Desire*, on the other hand, the same kind of line is mainly a device of characterization. Blanche reacts to the neighborhood in which her sister lives by saying, "Only Poe! Only Mr. Edgar Allan Poe!—could do it justice! Out there I suppose is the ghoul-haunted woodland of Weir!" Her slightly literary metaphor might well come from a high school English teacher, which Blanche has been, and the overstatement in it, the element of self-deprecation, is very much part of the character. Metaphor onstage, then, can be the playwright's pleasure, as in the speeches Fry put into Alizon's mouth; a character's mannerisms which help the audience identify her, as in Blanche's case; or two things at once, as with Ruth's "rat trap."

As with metaphor, so with symbol. Enid Bagnold's chalk garden, in the play of that name, is a playwright's symbol—an indication of the sterile and empty life of Mrs. St. Maugham. Although some of the lines, such as Miss Madrigal's "When will you learn you live on chalk?" seem to be about Mrs. St. Maugham's garden *and* her life, no character specifically identifies the garden as a symbol. That is left to the audience. In contrast, the sea gull in Chekhov's play with that name is a character's symbol. Three different characters talk about the sea gull as a symbol and, for all of them, it has a different meaning. For Treplev, who shoots it, it seems to stand for himself and for his unhappy love for Nina. For Nina, too, the sea gull is a personal symbol and she sees what happens to her in terms of the destruction of the gull. For Trigorin, who is a writer, the sea gull is simply an excuse for inventing a story. Chekhov never gives the sea gull specific symbolic meaning for the play as a whole. The wild duck in Ibsen's play of that name falls somewhere between the chalk garden and the sea gull. The duck has special meaning for the characters —a different one for each of them—and a meaning for the playwright as well.

When we consider how lines work in a play, how metaphor and symbol can be used, it becomes clear that the important thing about stage language is not its form but what it does. It is not something grafted onto the play. It carries the play. It is part of the characterization. It is part of the action. With the best playwrights, we do not listen to the words for their incidental beauty or truth, but because what really happens in the play is inextricably bound up with what the characters say.

6

The Language of Gesture

The stage's other language, gesture, can be as eloquent as the language of words. What a character does tells us as much about him as what he says. In most cases, we see a character before we hear him; the words, when they come, confirm or contradict the first, the visual impression. At the beginning of *Death of a Salesman*, Arthur Miller describes the entrance of Willy Loman: "Even as he crosses the stage to the doorway of the house, his exhaustion is apparent." It is Willy's walk, the sag of his shoulders, the tilt of his head that convey the exhaustion. This is the language of gesture. We learn, once the dialogue begins, that Willy is physically tired because he has inched his way home, driving a few miles an hour, desperately afraid that his inability to keep the car on the road will cause him to hurt someone. We learn before the play is over, that his fatigue goes much deeper, that he is worn out by a lifetime of trying and failing to achieve the kind of success he and his society admire. Willy is a complicated character, vacillating between doubt and certainty, between his longing to be "well liked" and his suspicion that he is laughable. For all his contradictions, however, there is nothing in Willy—not even his moments of wild enthusiasm—that contradicts our initial recognition of him as a man who is exhausted.

Miller cannot write Willy's walk as he does Willy's lines. He can only indicate the gesture, let us know the effect that he wants. Each actor who plays Willy must find the right way to move, the right way to stand to show us Willy's exhaustion, and each one will do it differently, will find his own gesture. In the last chapter, I pointed out that the meaning of a line depends on the way it is read. Some playwrights, recognizing this, use stage directions to indicate how they want lines spoken, as Miller does when he says that Willy speaks "with casual irritation" or Linda "very carefully, delicately." Even so, the reading of the line finally depends on the actor and the director. In performance, they contribute to a play's language. Where the language of gesture is concerned, where there is nothing so concrete as specific words on paper, their contribution is that much greater.

There are playwrights—Samuel Beckett, for instance— who spell out in detail what they expect the actors to do. Take the comic business with the ladder and the windows at the beginning of *Endgame*, movement so formal that it resembles a dance. Beckett is precise about what he wants.

> Clov goes and stands under window left. Stiff, staggering walk. He looks up at window left. He turns and looks at window right. He goes and stands under window right. He looks up at window right. He turns and looks at window left. He goes out, comes back immediately with a small stepladder, carries it over and sets it down under window left, gets up on it, draws back curtain. . . .

There is no point in quoting the entire stage direction, in following Clov as he gets up, gets down, moves the ladder; this sample is enough to indicate how meticulous Beckett is. He wants to fill the stage with deliberate movement which goes on and on in silence until the audience feels as though they ought to scream. The tension is part of the preparation for the first line, "Finished, it's finished, nearly finished, it must be nearly finished"; appropriately so, because the audience had about decided that it never would be.

Contrast this carefully described sequence with Launce's scene with the dog in *The Two Gentlemen of Verona* (Act II, Scene 3). Shakespeare, of course, does not describe what Launce does, since written stage directions were minimal in his day; detailed directions did not become popular until the nineteenth century. Besides, Shakespeare was part of the company which produced the play and could tell the actor what the scene demanded; he may even have written it to take advantage of a particular actor's comic talents. In any case, the stage direction is simply "Enter Launce." A later editor has added "leading a dog," unnecessarily since Launce's lines make it clear that there is a dog with him. The monologue is obviously designed to be delivered to the accompaniment of gesture— business with the dog, Launce's shoes, his staff, his hat—but the precise nature of that gesture is left to the actor. Sometimes an actor plays the scene with an imaginary dog, making it real to the audience by the way he behaves toward it. It would seem, then, that the actor's contribution to the creation of Launce is a great one, much greater than in the case of Clov. And yet, for all Beckett's explicitness, Clov's gesture depends on the actor, too. What, after all, does that "stiff, staggering walk" look like? One thing in my head, another in yours. It takes an actor to make it specific. In the discussion of the language of gesture in this chapter, I will refer to particular plays and to the effects in them that are visual rather than verbal. Most of the time, I will treat those effects as though they were the playwright's, but that is simply a convenient way of speaking. It is well to remember that when the play is in production, the playwright must depend on his collaborators—the actor and the director—to make the gesture that the scene demands.

It should be clear from the paragraphs above that I am using the word *gesture* in a broad sense, one that takes in not only the simplest hand movement—what we ordinarily mean when we say *gesture*—but also an extended act of some kind —what we mean when we call the visit of a head of state "a gesture of good will." So far as we are concerned in this chapter, a gesture is anything that an actor does on stage; it is what we see in the theater, rather than what we hear. It may be done silently or it may be done to the accompaniment of words. In either case, it may have meaning of its own; to understand a play fully, it is as necessary to recognize where and how the playwright expects a character to move as it is to understand what he says. I have used the word *business* in my earlier description of such stage activity. Where *gesture* is a general term, in which the stage meaning is not very different from the offstage meaning, *business* is more specific. Originally, it was a performer's word. An actor might say, "If I'm going to stand there through his long speech, I have to have some business," by which he would mean something to do with his hands—something to pick up, a pocket to put them in. In any ordinary Broadway comedy, the kind that plays summer stock and civic theaters a year or two after its New York run, there is an intense amount of business—lighting cigarettes, pouring drinks, opening purses, straightening ties, putting on lipstick. There is usually very little to these plays, and it is the business, presumably, that helps convince the audience and the actors that there is a little substance to the characters—at least their trivial acts are human.

There are some gestures which have a specific meaning to a group or a community—the Boy Scout salute, for instance, or the V for Victory which Winston Churchill made popular during World War II. Close your fist, extend your thumb, lift your arm so that it stands away from the body, move it slowly from left to right, making certain that the thumb points to the right. Every driver and every hitchhiker knows the meaning of that gesture. Other gestures are local. Once in a small Sicilian town, I came back after having a cup of coffee and found a man staring at my car. It was one of those odd, tall tin cans that Citroën makes, probably the cheapest car in Europe and practically unknown in Sicily. The man said nothing to me, but he slowly lifted his chin and, using his right hand, palm down, he stroked under his chin lightly, moving from the throat out. I had been in Sicily long enough to understand the language of gesture; he meant that he did not think much of my car. The list of gestures with a recognizable meaning in some community or other would fill pages; think, for instance, of the obscene gestures you know. All of these can be used by the playwright and the actor, insofar as they are known in the country for which the play is written or produced; since the audience understands them immediately, the playwright can save time that might have had to go to explanation. Such gestures can, of course, be used comically, so that the context makes a joke of the accepted meaning. Consider, for instance, how many movies, television shows, and plays you have seen in which a salute has become a gag; it is so used most often in scenes in which one character (the saluter) is making a mild protest at another character's bossiness.

There is another group of gestures, less formal than the ones described above, which are part of the vocabulary of the theater. They, too, are related to the gestures of real life. Perhaps the kiss belongs here; perhaps it belongs above because it, too, is a salute. I am thinking, however, of the gestures of sympathy in which one character indicates to another that he cares, that he understands, that he loves. At the end of J. P. Donleavy's *Fairy Tales of New York*, Charlotte Graves says to the hero, "I'm sorry." The stage direction calls for "A hand forward over Christian's hand." The words and the gesture say the same thing. In this particular play, the scene is a kind of joke, almost a parody of a sentimental scene, but it depends for its effect on the audience's recognizing a comforting gesture when the girl cups the man's hand in hers. A great many playwrights have used that gesture seriously and a great many more will. The manly hand on the shoulder is another such gesture; so, too, although less popular, is the cocked fist, twisted ever so slightly, the hint of the driving blow, which means, particularly if accompanied by a wink, "And remember, boy, I'm with you all the way." Just as there are sympathy gestures, there are gestures of anger, of fear, of passion. In a way, these are the clichés of acting, but they are as important to the playwright as those other clichés, the stock figures, because they provide him with the same kind of short cut. Such gestures only become banal when the playwright or the actor falls back on them for lack of knowing what to do. In knowledgeable hands, they can enrich a scene or a play.

Some gestures belong not to the world in general but to a particular person. These, which we call mannerisms or even tics if we are talking about our friends, can help the playwright with his characterization or help the actor give physical form to a character. Some performers develop mannerisms which are their own. With comedians, who usually play variations of themselves whatever part they play, this can be a virtue. Consider Charlie Chaplin's walk or the prim stare with which Jack Benny silently milks an audience for laughs. In a play, however, a performer's personal mannerisms may get in the way of the character. Take, as an example, Edward Everett Horton, a comedian who made a personal mannerism out of a stock stage gesture—the double take. A double take is a movement in which the character supposedly sees something unusual without its really registering, turns away, realizes suddenly what he has seen and whirls back in fascinated disbelief. A well-executed double take is almost always funny, and Horton is probably the best double-take artist in the recent history of American show business. He is also a talented comic actor, but as his mannerism developed, it became harder and harder for Horton to play any character who was not slightly befuddled, a little foolish, ready, at the drop of a surprise, to go into a double take. The mannerisms of a performer and a character can be the same, as they often were for the characters Horton played, and, when that is the case, the assigning of the role is called "type casting."

Where a play is not cast to type, the actor (sometimes with the playwright's stage directions to guide him) must find the mannerisms that suit the character. A good example is what Jason Robards, Jr., did with the part of Hickey in the 1956 off-Broadway revival of Eugene O'Neill's *The Iceman Cometh*. In his stage directions, O'Neill gives a physical description of Hickey (not at all like Robards), but his presentation of Hickey's manner is a very general one. It was up to Robards or the director (more likely, the two together) to come up with the mannerisms that would help identify O'Neill's character. Robards as Hickey jittered a great deal, was constantly in motion, and his hands moved continually, his fingers snapped a kind of jagged accompaniment to his nervousness. Through this activity, particularly the business with the hands, Robards could give us the surface of Hickey, the hail-fellow-well-met kind of salesman, always ready with a joke and a laugh. More important, however, he could suggest the pressure underneath, the turmoil and the incipient violence that had made Hickey a murderer. A playwright and his associates can thus use mannerism to tell us a great deal about character. Personal gesture can be used in other ways too—for instance, to let the audience know something that the characters themselves have not yet realized. The best example I can think of is from a movie rather than a play, a René Clément film, released in this country under several different titles, which I saw as *Lovers, Happy Lovers*. About a young Frenchman who has a way with the ladies but who really cares only about himself, the picture quickly establishes that the young man, whenever he is bored, pulls gently at his right ear lobe. In one scene, we see the hero and his new bride drive away from the church; when he leans back in the seat and tugs at his lobe, we know that the marriage he has just embarked on is not likely to be a very successful one.

As with the small movements, the mannerisms, so too with gestures in the large sense. These, too, can be either the trademark of the performer or the working tools of the playwright. It is with comedians, once again, that we associate specific gestures, comic routines that are identified with them. W. C. Fields, for instance, used to do a regular bit in which he attempted to put on his hat, got it caught on the point of his cane which he was holding up with his other hand and circled looking for the missing hat while it waved in the air beside him. Such a routine is part of a long comic tradition. It is a kind of *lazzo*, a name given to the byplay that went on in the *commedia dell'arte*, the popular Italian comedy that flourished three or four centuries ago. The plays given by the *commedia* were improvised, following a sketchy and usually familiar plot, in which an actor always played the same character. This specialization allowed him to develop his own routines—an elaborate way of eating spaghetti, perhaps, if he played one of the greedy servants—and audiences expected to see the routines, the *lazzi* that they associated with the particular performer. This kind of relationship between an actor and his audience was what I had in mind when I suggested earlier that Shakespeare may have put Launce's scene with the dog in *The Two Gentlemen of Verona* because it was the kind of routine that one of the company's comedians did well.

The scene with Launce really has very little to do with Shakespeare's comedy, except that it offers a momentary diversion from the play's other complications. The kind of gesture that we are most concerned with here, however, is that used by the playwright for a particular purpose. A fairly broad example can be found at the end of the first act of St. John Hankin's *The Return of the Prodigal*. We have spent the act meeting the leading characters and listening to a great deal of snobbish chatter from them, some of it referring to the ne'er-do-well son of the Jacksons, when Eustace is carried in, apparently dead or dying. Hankin gives his characters a first moment of hysterical concern, then contrives to get them offstage so that Eustace can play the scene described in the following stage direction:

The stage is left empty for a moment of all save the man on the sofa. Presently Eustace raises himself cautiously, looks round, then finding no one there takes off head bandage and wrings it out, listens again, then sits up and puts feet to ground, picks up a book with conspicuous red cover, on which he has been lying, glances at it, reads title, *Hester's Escape*, makes face, hears sound without, hurriedly puts feet up again on couch, replaces bandage, and lays his head back on pillow just as Mrs. Jackson re-enters with Henry.

On the simplest level, this extended gesture prepares the audience for the comedy in Eustace's sentimental awakening, "Is that you, Mother?" Beyond that, it provides a number of indications of his character—his flippancy, a certain degree of taste (he would not be reading a book called *Hester's Escape*), and, most important, a kind of hardness that lets him take what advantage he can, even of his mother, who is rather more kindly than the rest of his insufferable family.

Such a gesture is pure trick, collusion between the playwright and the audience to keep the characters from knowing more than they should. A more subtle use of gesture can be found in Henrik Ibsen's *Ghosts*, one that could tell something to the three characters involved if they were not too self-preoccupied to be as attentive as we in the audience are. Osvald, Mrs. Alving's artist son, has returned ill to his Norwegian home after living in Paris. His mother, who has come to the conclusion that she has wasted her life doing what was expected of her instead of what she wanted to do, is determined to see that he is happy. His happiness seems to depend, or so he thinks, on the pretty maid Regine, who is certainly not above thinking that Osvald is a steppingstone to a more comfortable and more amusing life than she can have as a servant. In the scene I have in mind, Mrs. Alving has so far given in to Osvald as to agree that Regine should join them in a glass of champagne. When Osvald invites her to sit down, she hesitates and "looks questioningly" at Mrs. Alving until the invitation is repeated. Then, according to the stage direction, "Regine sits on a chair by the dining room door, with the empty glass in her hand." Osvald and his mother then begin to discuss attitudes toward life and work in Norway and abroad while Regine sits silently, off to one side, still with no champagne; presumably—although here the stage directions stop and our imagination has to take over—she perches on the edge of the chair, wondering how she got into such a position. The business with the empty glass and the separate chair shows us that Regine is and will always be an outsider where Osvald and Mrs. Alving are concerned—not because the Alvings want her to be, certainly not because she is their servant, but because her self-concern is material and theirs, as the conversation indicates, is intellectual and spiritual.

Regine's physical separation from the other two characters, her taking the chair by the dining-room door, illustrates the way onstage space and the placing of actors in it can be used to show the audience something about the characters. Sometimes the playwright indicates where he wants characters to stand or when he wants them to cross the stage, but it is mainly the job of the director to see that the actors get in the right place at the right time. I remember a rather extreme example of positioning with a purpose in a production of Chekhov's *The Three Sisters* that Tyrone Guthrie directed at the theater in Minneapolis which bears his name. In Chekhov's play there is a character named Solyony, an army captain who, like most of the other local army officers, is a frequent visitor at the home of the three sisters. He is a difficult character, at once nasty and a little sad. He cannot bear to be away from the group when there is any kind of party going on, but he cannot take part; whenever he opens his mouth he is automatically rude, offending someone or starting a pointless argument. Guthrie illustrated Solyony's inability to be either in or out of the group by placing the Prozorov sitting room at the center of the stage (one that extends into the audience) and putting Solyony into a chair off by himself, on a finger of the stage that was far removed from the center of activity.

Another time, in a production of Luigi Pirandello's *Right You Are!* (*If You Think So*), I saw a director use the placing of actors to illustrate a point in the playwright's argument. Pirandello's play concerns a group of gossips in a small Italian town, determined to get to the bottom of conflicting stories about a new man in town whose peculiar behavior fascinates them. One character, Laudisi, remains outside the group— needling them, questioning them, reasoning with them, suggesting by all that he does that their search for the truth is not only not their business but is philosophically impossible. The director maneuvered his performers so that the gossips tended to form a cluster with Laudisi facing them from the other side of the stage. Not that their positions were set. There was a great deal of casual movement, nervous flutter when a new "fact" was brought in from outside, but inevitably the actors settled into the pattern of confrontation I have described.

In discussing the separation of Regine from the Alvings, of Solyony from the party, of Laudisi from the group, I have been careful to give reasoned (and, I hope reasonable) explanations for the spacing of the actors. I do not mean to suggest that an audience will react so intellectually to such spacing, but it will recognize the separateness of one character from the other. As the situation and the characters become clear, the visual impression may take on new meaning; even if some people in the audience never get to the point where they can say, "Regine is sitting there because . . . ," the visual separateness of the girl will have impressed itself on them and will help them understand her psychological and social separateness, which the play illustrates in many other ways. The gesture then—and spacing is a form of gesture—can say something specific, but it can also serve as a background and elicit a response from the spectator which will make him understand more clearly the scene or the play as a whole.

The play's other language is as necessary to it as words.

7

Sets and Props

The playwright, as the chapters on stage language have shown, can indicate what he hopes his play will do, but it takes the cooperation of the actor and the director before the effects materialize on stage. In the same way, the playwright in the contemporary theater must depend on the scene designer, the lighting engineer, the costume designer, the sound engineer, perhaps even the theater architect to give his play its fullest form. Each of these is a technician, working in a special discipline. Here we will be interested not in the technical problems—not in the way a revolving stage works or how a particular lighting effect can be obtained—but in the sets, props, costumes, lights, and sounds as they are used in the play. Special effects need concern us only as they do the playwright.

The set is a good place to begin. The range of possibilities here is tremendous. A play may be performed on a bare stage; it may be enacted within a set which is as nearly like the real thing as the scene designer and the carpenter can contrive. Although Samuel Beckett does not ask that the stage be completely bare, his *Waiting for Godot* is an example of the former. The stage direction says simply, "A country road. A tree." In both the productions I have seen (on Broadway and in a small theater near Philadelphia) the road was not depicted at all; the stage was the road, and a tree (abstract rather than realistic) shared space with the performers. The photograph on the front of the published English version of the play (Grove Press) suggests much the same setting, although the production is not identified. By contrast, listen to the description of the scenery for Act II of Eugene Walter's *The Easiest Way:*

> The dresser, which is up stage and C. against the flat, is in keeping with the general meanness, and its adornment consists of old post-cards stuck in between the mirror and its frame, with some well-worn veils and ribbons hung on the side. On the dresser is a pincushion, a bottle of cheap perfume, purple in color and nearly empty; a common crockery match-holder containing matches, which must be practicable; a handkerchief box, powder box and puff, rouge box and rouge paw, hand mirror, small alcohol curling-iron heater, which must also be practicable, as it is used in business of act; scissors, curling-tongs, hair comb and brush, and a small cheap picture of JOHN MADISON; a small work-box containing a thimble and thread, and stuck in the pincushion are a couple of needles threaded.*

This is only a very small sample. Walter goes on to describe the rest of the furniture—the "broken-down washstand," the

* The reading of plays involves the accumulation of a special vocabulary, although the meaning of most of the words and abbreviations is fairly obvious. *Upstage,* for instance, means at the rear of the stage; C. means center; and the *flat* is the set wall.

bed—and to continue his inventory of the cheap, worn, soiled paraphernalia that belongs to Laura Murdock, that expresses "the general decay of the entire room." Walter's play was produced in New York in 1908, at the time when the leading American playwrights and directors thought that the multiplication of realistic detail in sets made the play itself more realistic, more believable. Walter wants to indicate by her surroundings that his heroine has fallen on very evil days and that she is about to sacrifice her pure love for the absent John Madison to a rich man who will take her away from her poverty. The chaos and clutter of the room is a reflection of the confusion and despair in Laura herself. Although Samuel Beckett, writing almost a half-century later, is the opposite extreme from Eugene Walter, his setting, or the absence of it, is also a reflection of his characters. The two tramps waiting for Godot are nowhere in particular—and everywhere—and the stage's very bareness suggests the emptiness, the meaninglessness that the world represent for them.

The kind of set that tells us something about the play is a fairly recent development. At earlier periods in the history of drama, actors performed in front of conventional backgrounds which had only a generalized meaning. The Greeks, for instance, presumably acted their plays against a permanent backdrop suggesting a palace (for tragedy) or a street (for comedy). In most cases, in Greek plays the scene does not shift. In Aeschylus' *Agamemnon*, for instance, all the action takes place in front of the palace of Argos. The special character of that place will not be made clear by the generalized palace background; it will have to be communicated in the speeches. In the same way, all the encounters in Italian Renaissance comedy take place on the street; whether or not they all take place in exactly the same spot, the actors played them in a single setting, a conventional street running past conventional houses, in which the main characters supposedly live. In contrast to the Greek and the Italian Renaissance plays, in which the characters come and go, the Elizabethan plays shift the action easily from place to place. Each new scene is a new setting. When an audience at *Antony and Cleopatra* is asked to jump from Caesar's house in Rome (Act III, Scene 6) to Antony's camp at Actium (Scene 7) after less than a hundred lines of dialogue, we can be sure that Shakespeare is not depending on physical scenery to make the shift. If the presence of particular characters does not identify where we are, and if it is important to know where we are, the lines will tell us. Because of the speed with which scenes shift in Elizabethan plays, the theater itself was their only setting and it became whatever and wherever a particular scene demanded. Today, for instance, Shakespeare is usually acted against a neutral background—curtains perhaps—which might be anyplace.

If this were an historic account of scenic effects, it would be necessary to stop and consider the elaborate and expensive experiments that went on in Italy and England during the sixteenth and seventeenth centuries. In England, for instance, while the playhouses were practically scenery-free, there were court productions, called masques, which became excuses for complicated machines and rich decorative effects. Scenery as decoration, however, is not our concern here. It is scenery as a tool for the playwright that we are interested in and such scenery did not really come into its own until the nineteenth century. It manifested itself in the kind of preoccupation with realistic detail that the quotation from *The Easiest Way* illustrates. Its most important device was the box set which was first used on the London stage in the middle of the nineteenth century. The three-sided construction is now so familiar to us that it may be difficult to realize that it was once a revolutionary innovation. It put the actors inside the set instead of making them stand in front of a backdrop. It suggested a real room; it and the realistic furnishings that filled it were supposed to give the audience the impression that they were peeking through an invisible fourth wall into the private lives of the characters. I do not really suppose that audiences ever found the new sets quite that real, but the sense of actuality was probably a help to those playwrights in the last part of the nineteenth century who began to write seriously about contemporary social problems. An audience watching a woman move across what looked like a real kitchen and begin to wash real dishes might believe that her poverty or disease were real, too. That, at least, was what the advocates of stage realism thought.

The realistic set, however, brought more to the play-wright than a comfortable feeling that the surface of his play was working with his subject matter. It had and still has practical uses. When a curtain opens on a realistic set, the first step has been taken in telling the audience what the characters are like. We can guess from looking at the set something about their class, their economic status, their tastes. "The living-room at Rosmersholm, spacious, old-fashioned and comfortable." So begins the first stage direction to Henrik Ibsen's *Rosmersholm*. "A cavelike basement. A heavy vaulted ceiling, blackened with patches where the plaster has fallen off." So begins the first stage direction to Maxim Gorki's *The Lower Depths*. We may not know at first glance (that is, from reading the first sentence) what either of these plays is about, but we can guess—rightly—that *Rosmersholm* is not about people starving in a slum and that *The Lower Depths* is not a drawing-room comedy.

Not only does the set tell us certain things about the characters before we meet them, it can also reinforce things we learn about them after the play begins. Consider, for instance, some of the claims I made at the beginning of the chapter for the second-act set from *The Easiest Way*. It shows at once that Laura Murdock has fallen to an economic level much below the near-luxury she knew in Act I. It is not until the act is under way, however, that we recognize the clutter and untidiness in the room as indications of her desperation; as her state of mind becomes clear, the room seems more genuinely hers and it becomes a visual accompaniment to the action. The simple line from the *Rosmersholm* stage direction has also a suggestion of character. On the face of it, the sentence implies a settled, middle-class milieu and does no more than that. After we get into the play, however, we discover that a living room which is "old-fashioned" and "comfortable" may be a kind of statement about the play's protagonist. Two things contribute to Rosmer's difficulty in acting as his personal and political morality dictates. The first is Rosmersholm, the house itself and the family tradition that it represents ("old-fashioned"); the second is a self-indulgence within Rosmer himself ("comfortable").

I do not want to suggest that an audience in the theater reacts in so precise, so intellectual a way. I do think, however, that if a realistic set does the job that a playwright as subtle as Ibsen wants it to do, it should force the audience to react in two ways. At first glance, the spectator should feel "I know the kind of people who live there"; after he has been a while with both set and characters, his feeling ought to change to "The kind of people they are, I am not surprised they live there." The living room in *Rosmersholm*, then, begins by telling us something about Rosmer's status and ends by suggesting his character—that is, if the feel of the set approximates what is implied by the words *old-fashioned* and *comfortable*. Perhaps the best way of illustrating a vague idea like "the feel of the set" is to quote a scene designer explaining the feeling that he wanted his sets to establish. The play is Clifford Odets' *The Country Girl;* the designer is Boris Aronson. The play is about an alcoholic actor who is given a chance to play a big part for the first time in years. Much of it takes place in his dressing room in Boston, where the play is trying out and where it looks as though the pressures of his family life, his fear of failure and his self-doubt will send him back to the bottle. The last scene takes place in his New York dressing room and, in it, there is a tentative suggestion of rehabilitation. Odets makes no attempt to describe the two dressing rooms or to suggest that there is a difference between them. Aronson, writing in *Theatre Arts* (May 1952), explained the way he tried to differentiate between them, and why:

> I attempted to dramatize different things. The Boston one was very depressing: The beams overhead, the steam pipes showing and the walls broken down. That's because the play at that time is at its lowest point. . . . Finally, the most attractive setting, comparatively speaking, in color, proportion and design, was the last scene. This is where there's hope, where they succeed and can look forward to life confidently.

Aronson may have overstated the happy ending in this description, but he does indicate how two realistic sets, basically similar, can contribute contrasting moods to a play.

The illustrations in the last few paragraphs are from plays that call for realistic sets. It is necessary to point out that there are fewer of these each year. The realistic set had no sooner found its feet on the nineteenth-century stage than some playwrights began to resist it. While some men were developing it into the subtle device it can be in the hands of the best playwrights, others were trying to avoid it. There were two main reasons for these attempts to escape practicable doors and honest China teacups. The first was a practical reason, the second an esthetic one. The playwright quickly discovered that, however useful a tool the realistic set was, it was a brake on his imagination. Elaborate and heavily furnished sets took time to erect and, to escape the long wait between scenes (and some of the expense, as well), plays began to be written which were confined to a single set —or at least to a single set per act. Playwrights no longer had the freedom of Shakespeare; they could no longer jump from place to place with each scene. They had to find excuses for bringing their characters onstage in the first place, and excuses to clear the stage whenever two of the characters needed to play a scene in private. The box set, then, which began as a boon, became a burden. Its walls were knocked down and ways were found to suggest rather than depict actuality. Today's theater is full of such devices. There are moving stages that can bring on the corner of a room where a scene can be played; Phoebe and Henry Ephron's comedy *Take Her, She's Mine* was done that way—with the family living room sliding out of one wing and then sliding off while another set—the girl's dorm room, a coffee shop—came out the other side. There are multiple stages which have a number of playing areas, representing different parts of a house or places miles away from one another; *Death of a Salesman* was written so that its many scenes could be played on a single set with the audience's attention focused on first one, then another part of the stage. The heavy realistic set is still used on occasion, as in the New York production of *A Raisin in the Sun,* where the set itself was supposed to rein-

force the urgency in Miss Hansberry's lines. The devices
described above may rob the playwright of that kind of help,
but they do give him more fluidity.

They can also focus on the one important physical item
in a scene. In *Death of a Salesman*, for instance, when Willy
Loman goes to ask his boss to give him a job in the city, the
audience sees not a whole office but the barest suggestion of
an office with a tape recorder at the center of it; since the
purpose of the scene is to let us see the boss being indifferent
to Willy's troubles and at the same time sentimental about his
family on the tape recorder, emphasis on that machine is more
important to Miller's play than a realistic office would be. It
is here that the esthetic and practical reactions against realism
join forces. At first, it was assumed that realistic detail confirmed the presence of real emotions, but by the end of the
nineteenth century a few playwrights had begun to deny that
assumption. According to the new theory, the real truth, the
inner truth about man was obscured by realistic detail, and
it was the playwright's job to cut beneath the surface to
where dream and imagination, fantasy and hidden desires revealed what man was really like. Here is the last stage direction to August Strindberg's *The Dream Play*:

> She goes into the castle. Music is heard. The background is
> lit up by the burning castle and reveals a wall of human
> faces, questioning, grieving, despairing. As the castle breaks
> into flames, the bud on the roof opens into a gigantic chrys-
> anthemum flower.

Not exactly Laura Murdock's room in *The Easiest Way*, but
not altogether different either. For Strindberg, too, the set is
to contribute to the meaning of the play. In *The Dream Play*,
the daughter of Indra (the Hindu god of the heavens) comes
to earth to discover why there should be so much suffering

and lamentation on earth. She goes through a series of dream-like but painful adventures and then returns to heaven, leaving the earth only with what it had before—the hope or the longing to burst out of the restrictions of being human, to push toward the freedom of the heavens. The gigantic flower blossoming out of the burning castle and the wall of faces is supposed to be the visual presentation of that idea.

Between *The Dream Play* and *The Easiest Way* lies a whole range of plays that try to say something about man and the way he lives. Whether the play is blatantly realistic or insistently nonrealistic, whether it leans toward the former or the latter, the playwright can indicate that he wants a set which will contribute to his characterization, to his plot, to his milieu, to his mood, to his meaning. It is current fashion in the New York theater for the audience to applaud the set when the curtain opens. To my mind it is a foolish fashion. Until the play has run its course, no audience can know whether or not the set has done its job properly. A set that really contributes to a play deserves applause, but the set should wait—as the actors do—and take its curtain call at the end of the play.

The prop is an extension of the set. The term, which is short for *stage property*, takes in any physical object which is used on stage—anything that an actor carries, for instance, or that sits on a desk or table. As a general rule, any inanimate thing on stage that is not scenery or furniture or costume is called a prop. Size is not important. Clov's ladder in *Endgame* is a prop and so is Laura Murdock's curling iron in *The Easiest Way*. Here we will be less interested in what is or is not a prop than in how the playwright can make use of them. First, however, a warning about the misuse or the overuse of props.

A prop is not or should not be what its name implies. It is not something to lean on. In the chapter on gesture I mentioned those plays—popular comedies usually—in which there is a great deal of business which has no particular purpose. In such cases, the playwright and the actor fall back on props—cigarettes, cigarette lighters, glasses, bottles, cups, spoons, compacts, lipsticks, what have you—to give the characters something to do when the script is failing them. The prop should not be an excuse for meaningless activity onstage—even when it is a meaningless act that is often performed offstage. There are many legitimate ways for the playwright to make use of props.

A prop can be a plot device. The missing murder weapon, when it is finally found, is such a prop. So is the letter or the diary that gives away the heroine's terrible secret. So is the medicine bottle, the contents of which are so necessary to keep the old man alive. Let us take a specific example, however, and a rather unusual one—the prop that gives Edmund Wilson the title of his play, *The Little Blue Light*. It is a mysterious science-fiction kind of weapon, a ray gun of sorts that is set off by electrical waves sent out from the human brain when a person is overcome by a strong and ugly emotion—anger, jealousy, grief. It is shaped like a flashlight, and the bulb end lights up—a little blue light—whenever the weapon goes into operation. In the "not-remote future" in which Wilson's play takes place, we are to assume that a secret organization controls the world and that the play's protagonist, an irascible editor, is one of the few people still trying to expose and fight the secret tyranny. In the last act, a member of the organization brings in the weapon and the editor's wife, recognizing it, explains what it is and how it works, as much for the audience as for the other characters.

At the end of the play, the weapon is left lying on the mantel, facing the audience, which knows—although the characters do not—that the murderer has managed to turn the thing on before leaving. The end of the play, then, is a scene in which the three main characters, all of whom are against the secret organization, are unable to quit fighting among themselves. As they quarrel—getting angry, calming down, getting angry again—the audience can see the light go on, go off, go on, until at last it lights for good and the three characters are killed. The weapon, then, is a prop Wilson needs to illustrate his point about the destructiveness of human emotion. On a more ordinary level, it is a device to create tension in the audience. On both levels, it serves the action of the play.

A prop can be a characterization device. It makes a difference, certainly, whether a man carries a violin, a sawed-off shotgun, or a teddy bear. Seeing any of these might give us some hint of what the man is like. Probably the most famous characterization prop around today is not in a play or a movie or a television show, but in a comic strip. It is Linus' blanket in Charles M. Schulz' *Peanuts*. Any child who has a sister like Lucy to put up with is going to have to hold on to some prop for security; the blanket—which serves the same purpose for so many children—is a perfect choice for Linus. Not that the security blanket is a stranger to the stage. In the second act of J. P. Donleavy's *The Ginger Man*, Sebastian Dangerfield, trying to escape from both loneliness and an unpaid landlord, moves in on the wife who has left him. One of his first acts, after he sees that she will take him in, is to wrap himself in a blanket. "Get out of that blanket," she shouts, and he answers, "Just trying to store up a little security." At another point, taking up the blanket, he asks, "Would you mind, Miss Frost, if I wrapped up for dinner?" The American production of the play, taking its cue from these second-act lines, wrapped Sebastian in a blanket for most of the first act as well. Thus the playwright and the director used a prop to help indicate the defenselessness that lay just under Sebastian's aggressive surface.

A prop can be a symbol. Take the judge's gavel in Lynn Riggs' *Roadside*. This play is a fairly broad comedy, full of stock characters and standard gags, mostly designed to make the audience laugh and nothing more. There is one serious idea in the play, however, and that is that society—particularly the laws of society—is a force that cripples the spirit of adventure and freedom. Set in the Oklahoma Territory in 1905, the play presents a group of characters who outsmart or outbluff the law and take to the road in preference to settling down on a farm. The judge's gavel, which is first introduced into the play in a farcical courtroom scene, becomes the symbol of all that the main characters want to escape. "This thing represents the law," says Texas at the beginning of the last act, and he drops it into the campfire. At the end he fishes it out—charred now and partly gone—and offers it to the Marshal. "Course—it's kinda hot—and a little burnt on one end." The Marshal refuses to accept it (to arrest Texas, that is), the gavel goes back in the fire, and Texas and his friends take off in their wagon.

In the case of *Roadside*, the prop in question is a symbol to the characters themselves. A prop can, of course, be a symbol for the playwright and the audience without being one for the characters. An obvious example is the glass menagerie in Tennessee Williams' play of that name. Laura, the obsessively shy daughter in the play, is incapable of operating in the world. She has withdrawn into an isolated existence in which she plays old records and looks after her collection of glass animals. In one sense, these props may be seen as characterization devices, but the glass menagerie, itself, comes to symbolize Laura in the play; Williams makes this quite clear when he describes her as "like a piece of her own glass collection, too exquisitely fragile to move from the shelf." In the one attempt to move Laura from the shelf, the invitation to Jim O'Connor to come for dinner, the prop is used symbolically. Left alone with Jim, Laura overcomes her shyness enough to show him her collection, particularly the unicorn which is her favorite. Jim persuades her to dance with him and as they move clumsily about the room, the unicorn is knocked down and its horn broken off. "Now it is just like all the other horses," says Laura, adding, "Maybe it's a blessing in disguise." But Laura is wrong. Jim, who has been practicing amateur psychology on her with the best of intentions, does not know that you cannot make a horse out of a unicorn by knocking off its horn. After he goes, Laura sinks back into her menagerie. For Laura, her glass animals are a comfort, even a kind of occupation; for the audience the prop is a symbol.

8

Light and Sound

In the last chapter, I quoted—as an illustration of a non-realistic set—Strindberg's description of the stage effect he wanted for the end of *The Dream Play*. Let us recall two sentences: "The background is lit up by the burning castle . . ." and "Music is heard." Light and sound. Of these two elements, both of which can contribute to a stage effect, light is more closely bound up with setting since the total impact of a set depends in part on the way it is lit. There is something artificial about pulling either light or sound out of its total context—as there is in drawing a line between action and character. Still, for the sake of discussion, we will treat first light, then sound, as a separate element and consider the ways it can be used as an aid to the playwright.

Light has some very practical uses. In a play or an act which consists of a number of short scenes which are not going to be marked off by a closing curtain, the lights can be used to indicate where one scene ends and the next begins. This can be done two different ways. Either the lights can go out completely, using the moment of darkness as a mark of termination, or the lights can dim on one area of the stage and brighten on another. In Arthur Adamov's *Ping Pong*, a play in which a group of characters are totally absorbed in pinball machines, the author suggests the use of light as transition. The first scene takes place in a café in Paris, the second in an office. Toward the end of the first scene, the two young men who are the chief characters leave the café. At this point Adamov calls for "Darkness. Then two spotlights on Arthur and Victor standing downstage facing each other." They carry on their conversation in the spotlights while in the dark behind them the café is being replaced by the office. *Ping Pong* is not the kind of play which calls for heavily realistic sets, so the change involves little more than a shift in furniture which can be finished by the time Arthur and Victor decide to take their pinball ideas to the corporation office. They step out of the spotlights and into the new scene.

The methods I have described can be more than transitional devices. Take the full stop that comes when the stage is plunged into darkness. The playwright can count on that device's producing an effect on the audience, one that depends on what has been happening on stage, and he can use the expected audience reaction as one of his tools. Let us consider two completely different kinds of effect—one comic, one horrifying. First, the blackout sketch from a revue. This is a short comic scene which consists of some visual action followed by a single line and then by darkness. The slightly sick example which follows, which I made up for the occasion, may turn out not to be very funny, but at least it can indicate how the blackout sketch works. A woman, wearing a

shoulder purse, obviously drunk, staggers onstage and col-
lapses, falling down, her purse caught beneath her. A boy
walks on, looks at the prostrate woman, walks around her
cautiously, looks all around to see if anyone else is watching
and then stoops down and grasps the purse. He pulls at it. It
does not come loose. He pulls again. And again. The woman
does not stir so he rolls her over on her back. As he reaches
for the purse, he looks at the woman's face and says,
"Mother!!" Blackout. The line would probably not be funny
at all if its delivery was not followed by darkness; anything
that the audience was asked to watch beyond the line would
be anticlimax. Unless the action that an audience is watching
on stage has reached a natural conclusion, as happens at the
end of most acts and most plays, its interruption—by darkness
for instance—will be something of a shock. In the case I have
described, the shock of the darkness and the surprise of the
line reinforce one another; where no ending was expected
there is a sudden and very appropriate one. The result—the
sketch writer hopes—is laughter.

The other effect depends on the same audience expectation of the action continuing until it reaches a recognizable
conclusion. In this case the playwright uses darkness to blot
out the picture, but hopefully not to stop the action which
goes on in the minds of the audience. The insane killer closes
in on the child; the discovered murderer turns on the person
who has discovered him; the monster gets up from the mad
scientist's lab bench and heads for the heroine. Darkness.
Whatever horror the playwright might have put onstage, it
can hardly equal what the audience imagines—particularly if
there is a perceptible wait in the dark (with muffled sounds of
struggle onstage) before the house lights go up and the
audience goes out for a cigarette.

As with the blackout, so too with the business of dimming in one place, brightening in another. This involves more than mechanical transition. It can be a way of focusing the attention of the audience, a way of putting emphasis on a situation or a character. Sometimes, special lighting can make one character involved in an action stand out beyond the others. Since movement and speech are attention-getters, however, light as a pointer is more likely to be aimed at a person to one side, perhaps the person talked about. Take as an example the opening of Maxwell Anderson's *Anne of the Thousand Days*, a play about Anne Boleyn and her marriage to Henry VIII. Anderson opens with a Prologue in which Anne, shortly before her execution, considers her approaching death and the actions which brought her to this point. The actress playing the part sits in a spotlight and speaks a kind of soliloquy. When the first scene begins, a scene that takes us back to the time before Henry ever met Anne, it is played at the left side of the stage. The right side is not completely darkened, however; the light contracts until only Anne's face is visible. We see her for the first few moments of the new scene. What Anderson wants to do here is to use light to extend the effect of his Prologue beyond Anne's speech; he wants to remind the audience of Anne's end as we embark on the beginning of her story.

It becomes obvious, then, that lighting devices, even when they are doing the practical business of establishing transition, can operate to help the playwright elicit the audience response he wants. This, of course, is the function of lighting throughout a production. Light is used to do three basic things: to present fact, to establish mood, to act as symbol. The first of these is a relatively matter-of-fact process. The playwright can use the lighting equipment to tell us what time of day it is: daybreak, high noon, dusk. This was not always so, of course. In Shakespeare's theater, in which the plays were acted outside in the afternoon, it was the playwright's words that established the time of day. Horatio's famous lines at the end of the first scene of *Hamlet* let us know that day is breaking: "But, look, the morn, in russet mantle clad,/Walks o'er the dew of yon high eastern hill." True, the line does other things. It presents a metaphor that is attractive in its own right. It is a calming line after the flurry of excitement over seeing the ghost of Hamlet's father. But it does tell the audience that it is morning which means that the night watch is at an end which means, in turn, that the scene is at an end. The theater may have lost something verbally when lights could substitute for words to send the russet-clad morn over the eastern hill, but the substitution has pretty much been made. Now, a playwright is not likely to make a character comment on the morning unless the comment is designed not to tell the audience the time of day, but something about the character. Lynn Riggs' stage direction for the opening of Act II of *Roadside* begins "Dawn, the next morning," and he lets us know that "A faint grayish light steals into the woods." It is not Pap or Texas or Buzzey or any of the other characters who make Riggs' dawn; it is the electrician who sends the faint grayish light stealing across the stage.

The line between the factual presentation of the time of day and the establishment of mood is a thin one. If the lights dim so that we move from afternoon into early evening, we may also be settling into a feeling of peacefulness or a sense of foreboding, depending on the kind of play it is and how far along we are in the action. The quality of the lighting will help convey the kind of dusk it is—a gentle one or a frightening one. Similarly, there are hopeful dawns where the day breaks joyously and morning-after dawns in which the sun comes up with regret. A noon sun can warm or it can glare. A moon can spell romance for lovers or possible discovery for someone trying to escape. Thus not only the time of day but the way we are to feel about it can be communicated in the lighting. So, too, with the general lighting in the play. A dramatist may call for bright, hard light on his characters so that what they do can stand open, exposed, inescapable. He may ask for softness, dimness, the kind of light that shelters the characters if what he wants to do is to suggest something about them or to present them romantically or sentimentally. Sometimes we accuse a friend of being too starry-eyed about something—a girl, perhaps, or a job or a trip. We say, "You see her (or it) in such a romantic light." The phrase comes from stage lighting. If the playwright wants to be harshly realistic he will demand that kind of lighting; if he wants a romantic mood, he will bathe the stage with the light that helps provide it.

The third use of light—light as symbol—is less important than the other two, but it does turn up often enough to make mention of it worth while. Here is the stage direction that precedes the first entrance of the stranger in Jerome K. Jerome's *The Passing of the Third Floor Back:* "A beam of sunlight has softly stolen through the dingy fanlight. It lies across the room, growing in brightness." The play is a kind of sentimental Morality play in which the stranger moves into a cheap boardinghouse full of fools and villains and improves them all by showing them the virtues in themselves that they have not been able to see. Since the play is an English one dating from 1908 and since the Censorship would not let the figure of Christ be presented onstage, the stranger is never specifically identified as Christ. Still, Jerome means him to be Jesus, as a few of the lines suggest, and the light that introduces him is obviously symbolic. Since John, in his gospel, speaks of Christ as a light that "shineth in darkness" or that "is come into the world," Jerome is letting his symbolic lighting effect take advantage of a familiar Christian symbol. Similarly, a Nativity play might let a light shine out of the crib of the infant Jesus, suggesting the halo one almost always sees in paintings of the Madonna and Child.

Other instances of light as symbol tend to be more closely related to light as fact and as mood. Take dawn. It is not only a time of day (fact) and a posssibly joyous one (mood), but it can also be a new beginning (symbol). Thus, after characters have grappled with their problems through a long and desperate night and have reached the possibility of a solution, their play may end with a dawn which we are to take as new hope or the future or something positive and comforting. Not that the light symbol has to be dawn. Clifford Odets' *The Flowering Peach*—his play about Noah— ends, as did Noah's own voyage, with the rainbow, another symbolic light and again one borrowed from the Bible.

Mood or symbolic lighting is successful only insofar as it contributes to what the play is trying to do. For this reason, in reading a play, it is important to notice the kind of lighting the playwright calls for and to recognize its relation to the play as a whole. In the theater, we can only lean back and respond to the lighting, hoping that the playwright and the lighting engineer are working together.

Sound is the one theatrical effect that does not have to be onstage at all. It can be, of course. There is an old musical-comedy scene which was often used in the days when tap dancing was popular. A boy and a girl are onstage together, ostentatiously paying no attention to each other, because they have had the kind of meaningless quarrel that musical-comedy characters seem always to have. One of them—the boy probably—begins to tap softly, as though to himself. As he becomes involved in what he is doing, the taps become louder, the pattern more commanding. Reluctantly, almost as though she has no control over them, the girl's feet take up the rhythm the boy has begun. In a flash, the two of them are side by side, in the center of the stage, tapping cheerfully and, by the time the dance is over, the quarrel is over. This routine is a graphic if somewhat unusual illustration of the way onstage sound can be used as a communication between characters.

In most plays, characters have little opportunity to go into a dance, but there are other kinds of tapping—fingernails on tabletops, pencils on desks, playing cards on card tables—that can be signals between characters. The same kind of sound can also be a source of tension, if the tapping is presented as habitual to the tapper and a source of irritation to the character who hears it. Most of the sounds which originate onstage come from the actors and have some part in the presentation of the characters they portray. Of course, onstage sounds can come from the furniture or the set itself—doors and drawers that make noises when they are opened, rocking chairs that squeak when they are used. A playwright may use such devices to further his plot (think of mystery plays with noisy secret panels) or, perhaps, to get incidental comic effects.

The sounds that presumably emanate from the stage make up only a small part of the sound effects that are available to the playwright. The bulk of the sounds in the theater come from offstage somewhere—from the street outside the room where the characters are, or even from the imagination of one of the characters. On the most obvious level, sounds are facts, giving information to the audience. Accompanying the electrician's dawn that I described earlier for Lynn Riggs' *Roadside* is the sound of a rooster crowing. Riggs uses his off-stage rooster to make a joke, or a comment on Pap; Pap runs out following the second crowing and, after a "flurried squawk," he returns with a prop dead bird for breakfast. Before the rooster's untimely end, however, his crowing is a way for the playwright to let sound work with light to provide a dawn for the audience. More often, familiar offstage sounds contribute to plot; the sound of shots or the noise of an automobile starting or crashing can let the audience know what is going on. In Maxwell Anderson's *Winterset*, the two gangsters, Trock and Shadow, have a quarrel. When Shadow exits, he is followed by two men who have received a signal from Trock. The audience knows what to expect, but it is not until "Two or three shots are heard, then silence" that the expectation is confirmed. A similar sound device is used in Sidney Howard's *They Knew What They Wanted*. In the early part of the first act, much is made of Tony's nervousness and his drinking; so we expect that when he goes off to the station to meet his bride-to-be (the wedding was arranged by mail), there will be trouble with the car. The bride arrives on her own, having hitched a ride with the mailman, and as Tony's foreman tries to welcome her and calm her at once, the audience hears what it has been waiting for. "His words are lost in the roar of a Ford motor as it approaches," says the stage direction, "and the motor, in turn, is drowned in wild cries of dismay...." The sound here is not quite so specific as the gunshots in *Winterset*. We do not know that Tony has gone off the bridge until someone comes on to tell us, but we do know that there has been a wreck.

Sound can go beyond its contribution to a play's plot to help establish the mood or to feed the idea of a play. Take the business of the watchman's rattle in the second act of Chekhov's *Uncle Vanya*. This play, like most of Chekhov's plays, presents a group of characters on a country estate in Russia. All of them are disappointed, self-absorbed, a little desperate —afraid that they have somehow let life get away from them without ever having done anything. All during the second act, as one character after another reveals his unhappiness, the audience hears the rattle from somewhere outside. In one sense, this is a purely factual sound, a bit of local color. At this period in Russia, the watchman walked the estate at night, shaking his rattle, perhaps to indicate that all was well, perhaps to warn off anyone who should not be there. The noise of the rattle, then, ought to be some kind of comfort to the people who live on the estate. In *Uncle Vanya*, however, the estate is a kind of trap, a reminder for each character of his own sense of failure. For the audience, then, there is something ominous or sad about the noise of the rattle. I do not think that Chekhov intended the sound to mean anything specific, but as it recurs from time to time, punctuating the exchanges between characters, it becomes a reflection of their unhappiness. It certainly should suggest that to the audience when it is heard once again at the very end of the play.

In a Chekhov play, the characters, the lines, the props, the sounds can almost always be explained realistically, even though they sometimes—as with the rattle—take on a significance beyond the ordinary. In one instance, however, in *The Cherry Orchard*, Chekhov uses a sound effect which can only be symbolic; no realistic explanation is satisfactory. In that

play, Madame Ranevsky returns to Russia just in time to lose
her estate. She and her brother Gaev are incapable of action.
They talk aimlessly about trying to save the estate, but they
refuse to listen to the only practical advice they get. Lopahin,
a businessman who was once a serf on the estate, tells them
that they might save something for themselves out of their
situation if they chopped down the cherry orchard and cut
the land into lots for summer cottages. But Madame Ranevsky, like her cherry orchard, is doomed. At the end of the
play, the estate has been sold to Lopahin, the orchard is about
to be chopped down, and Madame Ranevsky and her family
are scattered. In the second act, as they sit talking, refusing
to face their problems, "Suddenly there is a sound in the distance, as if out of the sky, like the sound of a harp string
breaking, gradually and sadly dying away." Lyubov (Madame Ranevsky) asks, "What was that?"

Lopahin:	I don't know. Sounded like a cable broke in one of the mines. But it must've been a long way off.
Gaev:	Perhaps it was a bird . . . a heron, maybe.
Trofimov:	Or an owl. . . .
Lyubov (SHUDDERS):	Whatever it was, it sounded unpleasant. . . .

It is, of course, nothing so specific as the suggestions offered
above. It is a sound effect only, a device of Chekhov's to
emphasize what is going on in *The Cherry Orchard*. Madame
Ranevsky and all that she represents is dying out. The old
landowning class, inefficient and self-indulgent, is being replaced by the new businessmen, like Lopahin. The sound,
with its slow dying away is almost an aural illustration of
Madame Ranevsky and the inaction with which she faces

her loss. This becomes clear at the very end of the play when the sound is repeated, followed in this case, by "the sound of an axe striking a tree in the orchard." The axe is a real sound, like the watchman's rattle in *Uncle Vanya*, but here it is also symbolic, the sound of Lopahin's taking over.

Any discussion of sound as a mood device leads inevitably to a consideration of the use of music in plays. As with other sounds, the music can be made by characters onstage. In the Chekhov plays we have been discussing, there are characters who play and sing. Epihodov in *The Cherry Orchard* plays a very sad guitar and so does Telyegin in *Uncle Vanya*. In most plays, however, music is not made onstage. The incidental music a playwright calls for is one of his devices for commenting on the characters and the action. In *The Glass Menagerie*, for instance, Tennessee Williams wants a "single recurring tune . . . to give emotional emphasis to suitable passages." It should be like circus music, he says, heard at a distance: "It expresses the surface vivacity of life with the underlying strain of immutable and inexpressible sorrow." Although Williams says that the music is "primarily Laura's" and that it is used most clearly with her, the tune, as he describes it, seems designed to reinforce the general mood of the play. An example of music which does take on a specific identification can be found in *Death of a Salesman*. Arthur Miller's first stage direction for that play reads: "A melody is heard, played upon a flute. It is small and fine, telling of grass and trees and the horizon. The curtain rises." The immediate use of the music is to set up a contrast to the visual image we get when the curtain rises, the sense of enclosure which traps Willy in his neighborhood and his situation. At this point, the music suggests a general sense of escape or freedom or openness. As the play goes on, however, we learn that Willy's father was a flutemaker, a man who would not be bound by any conventional restrictions, not even those of the family. The flute is heard again, this time "a high, rollicking tune" as Willy and Ben discuss their father. The music of the flute, then, becomes more than a suggestion of a life freer, more open than the one Willy lives; it becomes specifically the music of the father who did choose such a life.

Tennessee Williams' *A Streetcar Named Desire* is a good play to use to illustrate the richness and complexity that can be achieved through the use of sound and music. The play is primarily the story of Blanche DuBois. When we meet Blanche at the beginning of the play, when she comes to stay with her sister in New Orleans, it is already clear that she is highly emotional and excessively nervous. Events in the play push her from her excitable state into real madness, and Williams calls for sound effects to indicate her increasing instability. At the beginning, we have two uses of sound—objective (that which is presumably real) and subjective (that which goes on in Blanche's head). The objective sounds include such things as the cries of street vendors, the screech of cats in the street, the noise of locomotives from the nearby rail yards and the music of a "blue piano" that comes from a barroom down the street. Blanche's violent reaction to the screech of a cat in Scene 1 indicates how her state intensifies sounds and prepares us, in part, for the sound effects of later scenes. The subjective sound is the polka tune, the "Varsouviana," which Blanche hears whenever she thinks of her dead husband. The tune is the one that the band was playing just before the young man shot himself. Since Blanche feels responsible for his having committed suicide, the tune haunts her. By Scene 10, in which Blanche is finally forced over the edge of sanity, the line between objective and subjective sound disappears. The cacophony that we hear is inside Blanche's head—imaginary sounds or real sounds turned grotesque and horrible by her fear. "The night is filled with inhuman voices like cries in a jungle. . . . The barely audible 'blue piano' begins to drum up louder. The sound of it turns into the roar of an approaching locomotive. . . . The inhuman jungle voices rise up. . . . The hot trumpet and drums from the Four Deuces sound loudly." The same kind of mixture continues, more muted, in the last scene, in which Blanche is taken away by the doctor and nurse.

Tennessee Williams, as *A Streetcar Named Desire* indicates, is one of the playwrights most aware of the way sound and music can help him get the effects he wants. Reading the play, we can see what he hopes the sound will do. In the theater, it is the composer and the sound technician who must make our ears see what our eyes have read on the page.

9

Costume

As any child who ever turned ghost on Halloween knows, costume and mask are instruments of disguise. As any child who ever turned ghost on Halloween knows, costume and mask are means of identification. As soon as he puts on the sheet with the eyeholes cut into it, the child disappears and the ghost emerges. The kind neighbor accepts the conventions of the game and recognizes that a sheet with eyeholes signifies a ghost. The masker is rewarded with candy or doughnuts and pennies for UNICEF and then, as likely as not, the sheet is lifted and the neighbor is allowed to see that it is a child after all. Costume and mask (or make-up, which is a variation of mask) work the same way in the theater. They disguise the actor and offer, in his place, a character. The audience accepts the conventions of the theater and recognizes the character that the costume signifies. The masker is rewarded with applause and takes his curtain call as himself—the actor seen through his disguise. For the play-wright, who must provide the actor with a character to play, the conventions of costume can offer a helping hand.

In the broadest sense, the conventions of costume extend beyond character and imply a whole theatrical genre. The sock and the buskin are the most obvious examples. The sock was the soft shoe worn by the comic actor in Greek and Roman times, and the buskin (or the cothurnus) was the thick-soled boot worn by the actor in Greek tragedy. Long after the actual shoes disappeared from the stage, the words *sock* and *buskin* were used to stand for comedy and tragedy. The words are less familiar today than they were a century ago, but a similar borrowing—visual rather than verbal—is still popular. I mean, of course, the masks of comedy and tragedy that we use so extensively as decoration—the smiling and frowning faces that we find on the front of programs and over the doors of theaters, on cufflinks and tie-pins, in adver-tisements and on souvenirs. Whenever an artist wants to represent the theater, he can always fall back on the twin masks, knowing that anyone who sees them will know what they mean—although the viewer may not stop to remember that they are the generalized descendants of the masks that performers actually wore in the Greek theater. A much more recent example of such a figure—a costume turned symbol—is that of the ballet dancer. The girl in the *tutu* (the short, flaring skirt), the long tights, and the toe shoes has come to stand for ballet itself and not for the character who originally wore the costume. It was apparently first worn by the heroine of *La Sylphide*, a romantic ballet from the early part of the nineteenth century, now no longer performed, but the present significance of the costume does not depend on its origin.

The masks of tragedy and comedy and the girl in the

tutu are reminders of how much the history of the theater has been bound up with costume. They are not, however, particularly useful in considering what the playwright stands to gain from the conventions of costume. To understand that, we will have to consider how costume is used to represent character offstage as well as on because the conventions of the stage are closely related to those of society. Let us begin with the most obvious kind of costume—the uniform. The soldier, the sailor, the policeman, the Boy Scout—all of these can be identified by their uniforms; the nun's habit is also a kind of uniform, as is the priest's collar, the judge's robes, the doctor's white coat. The uniform may tell us very little about the wearer as an individual, but it can indicate that he is one of a recognizable group, that he belongs to a particular organization, order, or profession. When a playwright wants to do no more than identify a character in that way—to let us know, for instance, that the man who walks onstage is a policeman —he can borrow the costume society already recognizes. He does not then have to take the time to explain that the policeman is a policeman, but he can let the character get on with what he has to do: make an arrest, get a laugh, get shot. The uniform thus becomes a short cut for the playwright.

Sometimes such a short cut implies more than just group or profession. During World War II, in movies and plays, the uniform of a German soldier (particularly an officer or an SS man) automatically identified the villain; similarly, the uniform of an American soldier, sailor or marine (particularly an enlisted man) elicited a sentimental response from the audience. Uniforms, then, can be used not only for group identification, but also for a very obvious kind of characterization which reflects attitudes of the society. A playwright who depends on such attitudes, however, is in danger of placing himself too solidly in a particular time or place, for attitudes change noticeably from country to country and from decade to decade. He is on safer ground if he builds into his play an attitude toward a particular kind of uniform—lets us know what the society within his play thinks of policemen or nuns or doctors—for then the audience can anticipate the response when a particular uniform appears without falling back on its own prejudices.

A kind of costume that is similar to the uniform as a means of identification is the national costume. The Arab's burnoose is such a costume, as is the American Indian's feathered headdress, the African's breechcloth, the German's *lederhosen*. The fact that the costume may be historical or ceremonial or even fictional is beside the point. Most American Indians today, unless performing for tourists, wear blue jeans or business suits or whatever the rest of us wear. This obvious fact does not do away with the feather as a theatrical or cinematic representation of the Indian. Most of these characteristic national costumes date from a period when countries were more insular, when each country imagined that all the others were quaint and foreign. Once, I suppose, Americans believed that all Japanese girls wore kimonos and carried paper parasols and that all Dutch girls wore wooden shoes and the peaked white cap that used to be on the Old Dutch Cleanser can. Communication is too good and too rapid for such beliefs to continue today. When Cho-Cho-San comes on stage in *Madame Butterfly*—either the 1900 play by David Belasco or the Puccini opera based on it—her costume identifies her. If an actress walks on stage in a Cho-Cho-San costume today, she may be supposed to be Japanese, but she may also be a kind of stage joke about the *Madame Butterfly* tradition of sentimental play. In either case, the playwright depends on the audience knowing what the national costume signifies and then reacting seriously or lightly, according to the situation. That such costumes no longer have a simple identifying meaning is another indication of the shifting societal attitudes I mentioned in the preceding paragraph.

There is a third kind of conventional costuming related to but less formal than either the group uniform or the national dress. This is the costume of the stock character. The sheeted ghost that opened this chapter is such a costume. So is the familiar tramp's outfit—the baggy coat and pants, the flapping shoes, the battered hat, the soiled white gloves, the blacking on the face to represent a growth of beard. So is the millionaire's morning coat, striped pants, and top hat. The tramp and the millionaire, as I have described them above, will be immediately familiar to most readers, but they imply once again not simply the character but an attitude toward what the character represents. No playwright today is likely to use these costumes in a play in which he deals realistically with either tramps or millionaires. Yet the costumes may have originated in reality. The tramp's costume may have been suggested by the kind of pick-up clothes that any itinerant derelict is likely to wear. Joe Fletcher in James A. Herne's *Margaret Fleming* (which dates in its original form from 1890) shows "from his battered hat to his spreading shoes the stains of the road." Joe is a comic character in the Herne play, but he is also supposed to be a realistic one and he is something of a tramp. In the nineteenth century, a tramp was still a possibly villainous character. Today he has become a slightly comic, slightly sad, representation of the outsider. He is a kind of symbol of that element in all of us which makes us want to resist the demands of society. As the character became symbolic rather than realistic, the costume became formal. Today, a playwright (or a performer) can use a tramp costume only for a comic or a pathetic effect: think of Judy Garland, dressed as a tramp, singing a sad song; or Red Skelton, as Freddie the Freeloader, performing his mime. As with the tramp, so with the millionaire. His costume is obviously an extension of the elegant dress of the last part of the nineteenth century. It may have been used once seriously to show that a character was a millionaire, but now it can only be used satirically.

I seem to have begun the last paragraph by describing the costumes of the tramp and the millionaire as those of stock characters and then to have spent the rest of the space denying my designation. And rightly so. The formalizing that I have described is another indication of the way changing times and changing attitudes affect the conventions of costuming. There is no costume that really represents a stock character. It is simply that, from time to time, the theater and its audience agree, informally, to accept a particular costume as representing a particular type. Pantalone, one of the characters in the *commedia dell'arte*, gets his name from his costume, the voluminous pants that were an exaggeration of the Venetian costume fashionable when the character was invented. Pantalone is the old man trying to be younger than his years, butt of a great many of the *commedia* jokes. That stock character has not disappeared. Whenever you see a comedy in which an old man courts a young girl and loses her to a boy her own age, you know that Pantalone is still around, although he no longer bears that name and he no longer wears the Venetian pantaloons by which seventeenth-century audiences recognized him as soon as he stepped onstage. Pantalone's pantaloons lasted a good long time, however

—a couple of centuries perhaps—longer, certainly, than the tramp's outfit and the millionaire's top hat have been around. It is probably safe to say that the kind of costume we are concerned with here begins by identifying a particular character, comes to stand for a type, finally becomes a convention in its own right and is used for special effects (Miss Garland's tramp song) and at last disappears, to be resurrected only for productions which want to evoke past centuries.

It might be easier to see this progression if we look at a conventional costume that is relatively new. Take that of the motorcyclist. We might begin with Frank Rooney's description from his short story "Cyclists' Raid," for that story, which appeared in *Harper's* in 1951, played a part in the development of the costume as we know it:

> Like all the others, he was dressed in a brown windbreaker, khaki shirt, khaki pants, and . . . wore dark calf-length boots. A cloth and leather helmet lay on the table . . . but he hadn't removed his flat green goggles, an accouterment giving him and the men in his troop the appearance of some tropical tribe with enormous semi-precious eyes, lidless and immovable.

There are two elements to this costume, one practical and one symbolic. Rooney's motorcyclists, like cyclists in reality, tend to dress in a way that offers minimum surface to the wind. Rooney's cyclists, even more than cyclists in reality, seem to be wearing a kind of uniform. Since his story, which is almost a political allegory, is about the way the cyclists terrorize a town, he emphasizes that they are a group and that they are frightening; both of these things are implied in his description of the goggles as a kind of tribal dress. In 1954, Stanley Kramer made a movie out of Rooney's story—*The Wild One*, which starred Marlon Brando. The costume changed slightly.

Perhaps taking a cue from Jean Cocteau's movie *Orphée* (1950), in which black-clad motorcyclists served as outriders for Death, Kramer dressed his cyclists in black—or in what passed for black in a noncolor movie. The familiar black leather jacket and the tight black trousers were born. Since costume is a two-way street, since the theater and the movies give costumes to as well as get them from society, many teenagers, aping Brando, went out and bought the right jacket. The first thing to go out of the costume was its ominousness. It never quite embodied the frightening antisocial quality implied in Rooney's story. It came to represent, instead, a young man, possibly delinquent, certainly in rebellion against his society. The emphasis, however, was on his youth and not his delinquency or his rebellion. For a time, the costume could be used seriously, as a designation for a particular kind of character. Very quickly, however, the costume became comic—onstage, at least. By 1956, when the musical *Bells Are Ringing* opened in New York, the authors could provide a comic number in which the show's heroine joined a chorus of black-jacketed young men to make fun of Brando, motorcycles, and the costume itself. Now, the costume is seldom used except as a joke. Here we have to stop, for what finally happens to the costume lies in the future. It might possibly develop formally, as the tramp costume did, but more than likely—considering the infrequency with which it is used now—it will simply disappear or lie dormant until 2010 when some dramatist decides to write a play about the quaint mores of the 1950s.

Although there are shifts in conventions and changes in meaning from decade to decade, from century to century, the playwright, operating at a particular time, can depend on his audience to recognize and respond to the conventions of that time. In the same way, a playwright, working in the realistic tradition, can expect his audience to understand the implications of differences in dress. Designers with a passion for historical accuracy sometimes dress Shakespeare revivals or plays with historical settings in the correct dress for whatever period is being depicted. The result may be attractive to the general audience, but it is doubtful that any but a few experts will be able to catch the nuances by which costume separates one character from another. In a contemporary setting, however, a great part of the audience will recognize the differences. Some of these will be quite obvious—those which separate the white-collar from the blue-collar worker, the rich from the poor, the young from the old. Others are a little more subtle, but a playwright can ask that his characters be dressed in a way to suggest that one is more conservative than another— or more old-fashioned, or more vulgar. In Gerhart Hauptmann's *The Rats*, for instance, he suggests that we can make a differentiation between two young women on the basis of the clothes they wear. One is a rather insipid middle-class girl, the heroine of a sentimental love story that forms the subplot of the play; the other is an excitable working-class girl, a husbandless young woman about to become a mother. Both of them, when we first meet them, are dressed to go out—the long dress, the hat, the parasol of the period—but we are told that the working-class girl is "vulgarly overdressed." Hauptmann hopes to suggest at first glance what will become clear as we watch the play—that the two girls have different backgrounds and different temperaments.

Hauptmann was a realistic playwright, at least when he wrote *The Rats*, and it would have been reasonable for him to assume that his audience could tell good taste from bad taste, the fashionable from the gaudy. It would have been reasonable, that is, had his play been offered to a contemporary audience. *The Rats* was written in the 1890s, however, and it was not produced in Berlin until 1911. By that time an audience might not be quite so sure what had been fashionable and what gaudy twenty years earlier. We would be even less certain if the play were produced today. Does this mean, then, that realistic costume is of no use to a playwright in suggesting character? Certainly not. Had *The Rats* been performed when it was written, the audience would probably have been able to use its knowledge of contemporary dress to put labels on the two girls. Still, their differences in dress do not lose their point because the play ceases to be a contemporary one and becomes a historical one, which means—from an audience standpoint—it ceases to be realistic and becomes imaginary. What replaces the contemporary audience's special knowledge is a context of costume provided by the play itself. In *The Rats*, as in any play, there is a suggestion of a standard, a correct way of dressing and any variation from it becomes a comment on character. Without really knowing the fashions of the time, we can recognize that the girl is "vulgarly overdressed" by looking at the other women on stage and remarking how she differs from them.

A playwright, then, can suggest that a character is too precious or too gross, too somber or too fastidious by suggesting the ways that his costume differs from the others. There is a kind of ugly-duckling play or movie in which, after a terrible initiation into society, the pretty young girl gains her self-assurance and becomes the belle of the season. There is a mandatory scene in such a play in which the girl goes to her first party. Perhaps she has no money to buy clothes with or no understanding mother to advise her. Perhaps she has been misled by the peer-group villainous who thinks it would be amusing to humiliate her. So she wears a floor-length white organdy with puffed sleeves while the other girls wear tight, knee-length black cocktail dresses, or she wears a simple after-noon dress with a Peter Pan collar while they wear taffeta ball gowns. In any case, she is very out of place and very upset. We, in the audience, do not need to know fashion from fondue to recognize the girl's plight and to respond with the proper lump in the throat.

Consider a similar scene. A group of men are sitting on-stage, dressed in business suits, mostly soft grays and browns. The door opens and a man enters, wearing a bright-green checked suit, a canary-yellow vest, and a derby. We do not have to be schooled in the correctness of the gray business suit to recognize that the derby-wearer is a touch vulgar under the circumstances. If the business suit is a little too close to us to make the point clearly, think for a moment of Restoration comedy. By our standards, all of the sparks of the period dressed rather outrageously—not only bright-colored coats and breeches of rich materials, but wigs as well. In each of the plays, however, there is a character, the fop, who dresses much more ostentatiously than the others. Perhaps when the plays were first produced, the fashionable audience could recognize the fop because they knew what ribbons were in and what laces were out. But we have no problem with Restoration revivals today. There are degrees of gaudiness, and, although all the young men in George Etherege's *The Man of Mode* may be peacocks to our dull eyes, when Sir Fopling Flutter walks onstage the contrast is apparent. Even among extrava-gant costumes, inane extravagance stands out.

So far we have been considering costume as a characteriz-ing device. That is its primary function, but playwrights oc-casionally use costume for other effects in plays. It might be valuable here to look at a few examples. Let us begin with

A Streetcar Named Desire. Tennessee Williams describes Blanche when she first walks on stage:

> She is daintily dressed in a white suit with a fluffy bodice, necklace and earrings of pearl, white gloves and hat, looking as if she were arriving at a summer tea. . . .

The whiteness, the daintiness of the costume is suitable for the character of Blanche, who likes to think of herself that way, but Williams is doing more than indicating something about his heroine. The important thing about the costume, as Williams points out, is that it separates Blanche from the surroundings: "Her appearance is incongruous in this setting." Blanche is going to be destroyed by the end of the play and Williams wants her first appearance (she "suggests a moth") to imply that end. Costume here becomes a way of foreshadowing the events to come.

Costume, or changes in costume, can also be used to reinforce the action as it takes place. Eugene O'Neill's *The Emperor Jones* is a good example. When we first see Jones, he is wearing an elaborate uniform, heavy with gold braid and brass buttons. At that time, he is the self-appointed emperor of an island in the West Indies and his costume is an indication of his position. His subjects have grown tired of him and of the way he milks them for his own advantage. As the play begins, a revolution is afoot and Emperor Jones is ready to leave the country, to go back to the United States and live on what he has made out of being emperor. To escape, however, Jones must pass through a great forest, and the play is about what happens to him in that forest—how superstition and fear overcome him and turn him into a frightened savage. It becomes quickly clear that his fancy uniform is not only an indication of his office, but a symbol of the veneer of civilization that overlays the primitive man. By Scene 3 he has lost his hat and his uniform is torn; in Scene 4 he throws away his coat and his spurs; in Scene 5 he discards his shoes and his pants are in tatters; by Scene 6 he looks as though he is wearing a breech cloth. It is quite obvious that O'Neill wants to show visually, through costume, what is happening to Jones; he is stripped physically as he is stripped psychologically. At the end, just before he is killed, Jones is as naked as the stage will allow, and he has become primitive man again.

As Eugene O'Neill uses the ripping away of costume to illustrate his action, so Bertolt Brecht, in *Galileo*, has a character dress onstage to make an important point. In the Brecht play, the authorities, primarily those of the church, oppose the experiments of Galileo. They do so because they are afraid that if Galileo upsets accepted ideas about the heavens, his scientific revolution might lead to social and political revolution, and thus endanger the power of the church. Individual members of the church hierarchy, however, are sympathetic to Galileo and his experiments. One of these is Cardinal Barberini. In the course of the play, Barberini becomes Pope, but Galileo learns to his disappointment that his old supporter has become his new enemy. Brecht's point is that the church and Galileo are necessary opponents and that Barberini, in becoming head of the church, can no longer think or act as an individual. He must accept the pressures of the church itself. Brecht shows this in a dressing scene in which Barberini is being robed with the vestments of his new office. As he is being dressed, he argues with an Inquisitor who wants to arrest Galileo. His arguments become weaker with the addition of each new part of the costume. By the end of the scene, he is fully dressed. He has ceased to be Barberini and has become the Pope. He consents to the Inquisitor's demands. Brecht's use of costume in this play is among the most effective on the stage. Changes of costume are often used by playwrights to indicate shifts in character or situation, but when the change is made onstage the effect on the audience is much more immediate.

Sometimes, as one comes out of a theater, one can hear a woman in the crowd say, "I didn't like the play much but she wore gorgeous clothes." If the play is a musical or a historical drama or a Shakespeare revival—any production in which colorful costumes are possible—the remarks about how attractively dressed the show was are likely to be more frequent—and not simply from women. One of the legitimate uses of costume onstage is to delight the eye of the beholder. Even Aristole said that Spectacle (which includes costume) is one of the six necessary elements of tragedy. In this chapter, however, we have considered costume in relation to the play and not to the physical production, from the standpoint of the playwright and not the designer. Beautiful costumes are always a pleasure in the theater, but the best costumes are not necessarily the most beautiful. Costume is doing its job properly when it combines beauty and purpose and performs some function within the play.

10

Theater and Stage

It would be difficult to imagine the variety of circumstances under which productions of *Hamlet* have taken place in the centuries since it was first produced. It has been given in outdoor amphitheaters and on improvised platforms in church basements, in living rooms and lecture halls and conventional theaters, on steamboats and from the back of caravans, in puppet theaters and opera houses, in the movies and on television. A play, once it is written, passes out of the playwright's hands and, if it remains popular, it is likely to be produced in ways he never imagined. Still, while he is writing the play, the dramatist ordinarily has a particular theater or a particular kind of theater in mind. The play is likely to bear the marks of that theater. *Hamlet*, presumably, was written for the conventional theater of Shakespeare's time. It would have been performed on a stage that jutted into the audience which stood on three sides of the action. There was practically no scenery, except perhaps on the inner stage—a small area at the rear of the main stage which could be closed off by a curtain. Since the play was performed in the afternoon, under the open sky, there were no lights and, hence, no lighting effects. Of the mechanical aids to the playwright discussed in the last few chapters, only sound and costume were available to Shakespeare. Still, if Shakespeare could not use scenery to get effects as later dramatists could, he was not burdened by it either. The quick shifts in scene which give *Hamlet* or any of Shakespeare's plays pace and richness are partly a result of the kind of theater for which he wrote. The stage, then, and the theater building itself are part of the playwright's tools.

In this book, we are primarily interested in how to read and understand a play. A particular stage or theater building may have helped dictate the form that a play takes, but it is the form and not the process that we are concerned with here. Still, it is probably worth while to take a few pages to consider the problems of theaters and stages. A theater may be any shape and almost any size. The shape need not detain us, since it is the way the stage is set up inside that counts, but size is important. A playwright for a theater that seats two hundred people can use more subtle effects than one who writes for a theater that seats two thousand. The larger the theater, the broader the gesture has to be. The broader the gesture, the simpler the emotion which is supposed to elicit it. If you read through a collection of nineteenth-century English plays, you will find that there is practically no subtlety of characterization, that the action is broad and the situations obvious. One reason for this is that the theaters of that time were mostly very large and the plays written for them had to be easily understood in the farthest balcony. It is significant that T. W. Robertson, who took the first steps toward the realistic writing of plays in England, wrote for a company which acted in a relatively small theater, for which they had to develop a more natural acting style. Today, on Broadway, the largest theaters house the musical comedies. The musicals fit comfortably in such theaters because the characters and situations are for the most part uncomplicated and can be communicated through overstated gestures which the music makes acceptable. For the same reason, opera houses are large. There may be subtlety in the music of an opera, but the story it tells is not likely to be shot through with suggestions and nuance.

This division between the large and the small theater, between the obvious and the subtle play is a fair one, but perhaps it should be softened a little. The division might be said to be between the natural and the formal gesture. If a playwright wants to suggest a relationship between two characters by the way each reacts to what the other says, he has to make certain that his audience sees that reaction. In a small theater, he can ask for little more than a lifted eyebrow, a half-look. In a large theater, he may have to ask for a grimace and the lifting of hands. The former gesture may be a natural one, with meaning in its context; the latter is more often a formal one, one of a group of gestures which the audience has learned to recognize as dismay or horror or surprise. Stuck with a stock gesture of horror, the playwright is likely to write a stock character with a stock emotion to express it. It is in this way that the size of a theater is likely to effect a play's subtlety.

Not that subtle plays cannot be written for large theaters. The Greek tragedies have fascinated readers for years with their suggestivity and yet they were performed in vast amphitheaters, some of them—such as the one in Epidaurus—seating 16,000 people. The actors wore masks and costumes that made them larger than life and high-soled shoes which apparently made natural movements impossible. The choruses sang their speeches and danced to them to set patterns. Once again, then, the gesture was formal. Since there was never a question of realistic acting, the playwright could use the conventions of his theater, which were grandiloquent, and whatever subtlety he had could be confined to his verse. In this sense, there is a kind of comparison with opera which, until recently, was hardly acted at all; the emotions were depicted in standard poses and confrontations—the tenor and soprano approaching one another, arms outstretched, shouting their heads off—but the conventions were given color and richness through the music.

The stage, even more than the theater itself, is likely to affect the form of a play—or at least the devices of which it makes use. The standard stage of our time is the one that you can see in any Broadway theater and in any high school auditorium. It is a raised platform which backs away from an audience, goes into a kind of hole. It is called the proscenium, or the picture-frame, stage. The word *proscenium* is borrowed from the arch which rises at the front of the stage, separating it from the auditorium. *Picture-frame* is self-evident; watching a play on a proscenium stage is a little like looking at an animated picture through a frame. The virtues of this kind of stage, as suggested in the chapter on sets, is that it is the best place to build realistic scenery, to give the audience the idea that it is looking at an actual room. A playwright striving for such actuality found an ally in the stage. A playwright who wanted more imaginative effects found an enemy, for the proscenium stage's greatest drawback is that it hems in the action, restricts movement. A great many mechanical devices—

revolving stages, treadmills, area lighting—were invented to combat the restrictions. Even so, most of the plays of the modern theater were written with the proscenium stage in mind. This is obvious in the realistic plays in which the playwright carefully sets his stage for a particular effect. It is just as obvious, however, in a play like Strindberg's *The Dream Play*, which called for a completely unrealistic set; even though it was protesting the confining quality of the proscenium stage, the play was plainly conceived as a picture at which the audience looks.

It became clear to workers in the theater—to directors and actors even more than to playwrights—that the most characteristic thing about the proscenium stage was that the arch itself separated the audience from the actors. They felt that an artificial barrier had been set up between the play and the people who had come to see it and that the footlights and the orchestra pit increased the size of the great divide. In earlier times, it was remembered, the audience and the actor were closer together—in the Middle Ages when the plays were performed from carts in the market square, in the Elizabethan age when inn-yards and then theaters built on the model of the inn-yard put the action in the midst of the audience. The first step was to break through the proscenium, to reach out toward the audience. This was done through various kinds of extended stage. The apron stage is one example; an arc that reaches out across the orchestra pit, it lets some scenes be played much closer to the audience than the proscenium would have permitted and with no scenery at all. The runway is a more exotic example; it extended out over the first several rows in burlesque houses, bringing the girls that much closer to the customers in the best seats.

Playwrights also began to worry about the division between actors and audience and to get around it by writing plays which spilled over into the auditorium. Luigi Pirandello's *Tonight We Improvise* is an example. The play is about the putting on of a play, and the director of the play-within-the-play enters through the auditorium, climbs up on the stage and begins to address the audience directly. Scattered here and there through the audience are other members of the cast, who comment on the action or argue with the director. Some action takes place in the lobby during the intermission. In his play, Pirandello is concerned, as he usually is, with the problem of what is truth and what is illusion. His tricks then are not simply attempts to escape the proscenium stage. They are also valid illustrations of his main theme. Thus, they become efforts to use the proscenium stage in a way that will violate its basic premise—that there is an invisible wall hanging up there between the auditorium and the stage.

Apron stages and plants in the audience, however, are really only makeshifts that cling to the proscenium stage. The real attack on that stage came in the movement toward the open stage which has been strong, in the United States at least, for the past thirty years. Its first and most revolutionary manifestation began in the universities. That was the arena stage or the theater-in-the-round which was first used extensively by Glenn Hughes at the University of Washington. With such staging, the audience sits in a circle around the playing area,* which is often on the same level as that on which the audience sits. Under such circumstances, scenery is impossible, since it would shut off part of the audience from the action, and furniture is minimal. The intimacy of such a theater de-

---

* The strangest variation on this that I have ever heard of was Albert Camus' production of his first play, *Revolt in the Asturias*, in 1936. He put the spectators in the center and had the actors perform all around them. He wanted the audience to feel that they were really *in* the town of Oviedo.

pends on the proximity between the actor and the man looking at him and not on an artificial contrivance that tries to
force the observer to think of himself as a performer, as in the
Pirandello situation. The theater-in-the-round was particularly
popular in this country in the years immediately following
World War II, partly because it was a relatively inexpensive
kind of stage to set up. Arenas bloomed then in many cities,
mostly in abandoned night clubs and on hotel dance floors.
This initial popularity has now died down, although there are
still a great many theaters-in-the-round in this country, the
most famous of which is Arena Stage in Washington, D.C.

The decline in popularity of the theater-in-the-round
does not mean that the opponents of the proscenium stage
have given up. It is simply that the full arena has been eclipsed
by another kind of open stage, one which does away with the
proscenium arch but holds on to the back wall where limited
scenic effects can be used. It is basically a modification of the
Elizabethan theater which allows the audience to surround the
action on three sides, putting them closer to the performances.
Tyrone Guthrie, the English director, is probably the one
man most responsible for the increasing acceptance of this
kind of stage. He experimented with it at the Edinburgh Festival in 1948, but it was the success of the Shakespeare Festival
Theatre in Stratford, Ontario, that proved the effectiveness
of such a stage. Variations on this kind of open stage can now
be found at the Chichester Festival Theatre in England, the
Tyrone Guthrie Theatre in Minneapolis and the new Repertory Theater of Lincoln Center in New York. All of these
stages differ, of course, but what they have in common is the
possibility of a greater fluidity in production, made possible
by the removal of the restricting proscenium and the increase
in the number of paths by which the actors can enter and

exit. That, and a closer connection between the audience and the actors.

The advocates of the open stage are occasionally too enthusiastic about it. It, too, has its limitations. Plays written for the proscenium stage have been adapted to the arena or three-sided stage, but not with uniformly happy results. On an open stage, the actors must keep moving so that no part of the audience has to look too long at any particular back. This imposed movement can do harm to a particular scene, one written by the playwright with the traditional picture frame in mind. Take the scene in the first act of Ibsen's *Hedda Gabler*, in which Hedda decides to charm Mrs. Elvsted. Hedda, with her strong sense of her own superiority, is friendly to Mrs. Elvsted only to find out what she wants to know. From the scene, the audience should get a sense of Hedda's insincerity and her contempt for Mrs. Elvsted, but also a recognition that Hedda can be socially charming when she wants to; the audience must also see Mrs. Elvsted's fear and suspicion and, finally, her relief in having apparently found a friend. A certain amount of bustling about might be possible on Hedda's part, but the movement in the scene is pretty much restricted to her pushing a footstool close to Mrs. Elvsted; the force of the scene is built on the delivery of lines and the reaction to them. Although the scene can be played on any kind of stage, it was obviously designed for the traditional proscenium which lets the audience face both women at once, and it would lose some of its force on an open stage. The work of Ibsen, then, bears the marks of the theater he wrote for, and so does the work of the best of the early modern dramatists—Strindberg, Shaw, Chekhov. What is good for Shakespeare is not necessarily good for Ibsen, and some theatrical architects have begun to recognize that fact. Theaters are being designed now that can be converted—through movable seats, stages, arches—into theaters-in-the-round, three-sided open stages, or traditional prosceniums.

The convertible theater is still a comparative stranger in this country. The building of most theaters seems to require a choice of one kind of stage over another. If the movement toward the open stage continues, presumably the playwrights will begin to write plays with that kind of stage in mind. There has been little evidence of this so far. One reason is that there has been little new American writing for any stages away from Broadway. Most of the arenas use a conventional repertory, part classics and part Broadway successes. The theater-in-the-round that Margo Jones ran in Dallas in the late 1940s did make an effort to introduce new works and new playwrights. The best-known works that came out of that venture are probably Tennessee Williams' *Summer and Smoke* and William Inge's *Farther Off from Heaven* (which eventually became *The Dark at the Top of the Stairs*). As we know these works, which is from the New York rather than the Dallas versions, they are plainly proscenium plays; Williams', for instance, calls for an elaborate symbolic set which is described head-on. If the plays in an earlier version indicated their arena origins, the revisions do not show it. Until the opening of the Lincoln Center Repertory, the three-sided open stage had been pretty much limited to festival theaters, committed to classical repertory (mostly Shakespeare), and not to the presentation of new plays. Arthur Miller's *After the Fall*, the first play for the Lincoln Center, seems designed to take full advantage of the open stage, allowing for action in more than one place at once. While the hero talks directly to the audience, a character or a scene he recalls can be seen on another part of the stage. Miller, of course, had tried to do something similar in *Death of a Salesman* and there he had suggested that the stage be pushed out into the auditorium. In *After the Fall*, he has escaped the proscenium completely and the form of the play shows his escape.

A recognition that a particular kind of stage or theater is likely to affect the way a play is written is useful as one reads a play and imagines it in production. When we stage it in our heads we can put up the proscenium or take it down according to the demands of the play, for the imagination is an inexpensive convertible theater.

11

Yes, But What's It All Mean?

From time to time in the preceding chapters, I have used the word *idea*—casually, as though all my readers would know what I meant by a phrase like *the idea of the play*. And so they do, I suppose. Still, there is a problem about meaning in plays and it might be well to give a few pages to a consideration of those somewhat amorphous terms: *meaning, idea, theme, message, thesis*.

At the beginning of Chapter 3, the chapter on *action*, I pointed out that the two questions most often asked about a play are "What happened?" and "What's it about?" I suggested that the two questions are pretty much one—at least when asked and answered in an offhand way. There is a difference between them, however. The answer to "What happened?" is a description of the play's action. The answer to "What's it about?" is a statement of the idea embodied in the action—the *theme*, to use the most popular technical term.

The problem mentioned in the first paragraph is one of differentiating between the action and the theme. With some playwrights there is no difficulty at all. Some dramatists tend to think of the theater as a lecture hall in which they can teach, persuade, urge the audience to behave in a particular way. In such cases the action of the play is of less importance than its idea; the action is simply a vehicle for the idea, an illustration to get the point across. On the simplest level, such plays are merely propaganda, put out by a particular group (sometimes the government of a country or a city) to teach a lesson. A few examples will indicate what I mean. In 1952, Lee Maryat wrote a play called *Dope*, which was put on by the East Harlem Protestant Parish in vacant lots in that part of Manhattan; it was a warning of the consequences of taking a first shot of dope. In 1953, the Reverend Philip W. Turner, who then had a parish in Leeds, wrote a play called *The Christ in the Concrete City*, which was to be performed in factories in the industrial areas of England; it was designed as a converting play, to bring the workers into or back into the church. In a Supplement on Chinese literature (December 1959), the *Atlantic Monthly* published Fang Tzu's *Do Not Spit at Random*, a play written for production on street corners; it was part of a sanitation drive of the Chinese government, and it was supposed to teach that spitting on the streets is both unsanitary and antisocial. In the case of plays like these, *idea* and *theme* are inappropriate words. These plays are *messages*.

There are other *message* plays that do not demand that an audience do anything quite so specific as join a church, avoid taking dope, or quit spitting on the street. These can, however, be direct appeals to an audience to support a particular political party or program. Clifford Odets' *Waiting for Lefty*, one of the best-known American plays of the 1930s, is such a play. The main action of the play is a union meeting of taxi drivers in which the rank-and-file members defy their corrupt officers and go out on strike; there are a number of scenes which interrupt the meeting to show the background of the strike, the economic conditions that have made it necessary. The play is designed not only to call for the audience sympathy for strikes, but also to suggest that the best solution for the workers lies in the Communist party. Such a play, in its direct attempt to peddle a political idea, presents an obvious message.

There is still another kind of message play which is a little less blatant. This is the *thesis* play. In it, the playwright takes as his subject some social problem and, by means of his play's action, manages to illustrate the correct attitude (that is, his own) toward the problem. In this category, we find the pacifist plays which illustrate that war is both pointless and horrible. Here, too, are the prison-reform plays which insist that imprisonment should be therapy not punishment. Here, too, are the double-standard plays, so popular in the 1890s in England, in which the playwrights insisted that wives and husbands should have the same rights in marriage. The possibilities for the thesis play are as many as the problems that face any society. Playwrights can use their plays to suggest (or to insist) that audiences would do well to alter their attitudes toward juvenile delinquency or capital punishment, toward the place of the Negro in society, toward the treatment of mental cases or the relation of parents to children. Whatever his thesis, a playwright can find a story to present it.

When the playwright uses his play as a propaganda device or a teaching aid, when his theme is reduced to a message or a thesis, there is no problem. The question "What's it about?" can be answered simply. It's about the need for better schools, we might say, or about the dangers of the atom bomb. When the playwright is working as an artist, however, rather than as a propagandist, it is not so easy to separate the theme from the action. In fact, the very act of separation offends some playwrights. In this, they share the concern of other artists, both literary and nonliterary—novelists, poets, composers, painters. There is a story about a composer who played his latest work for a group of friends. When he had finished, one of them, who probably did not remain his friend long, said, "It's lovely, but what exactly does it mean?" The composer sat back down at the piano, played the piece through again and then said, "That's what it means." Archibald MacLeish stated the case for the artist most emphatically in his famous poem "Ars Poetica," which ends:

> A poem should not mean
> But be.*

Although the last lines of MacLeish's poem are often quoted to emphasize the falsity of confusing form with content (*action with idea,* in the terms I have been using with the drama), they disprove as much as they prove. It is obvious that "Ars Poetica" not only exists as a poem, but has something to say about the nature of poetry—has a meaning, then, that can be paraphrased, stated outside the poem itself. Although any work of art has a meaning, the artist is understandably leery of having that meaning stated baldly. The writer obviously and justifiably does not want a complicated work reduced to a few easy words.

The artist's hesitancy in the face of defining the ideas in his work can be illustrated by the comments of two men, one

* From "Ars Poetica," by Archibald MacLeish, by permission of Houghton Mifflin and Company.

a movie director, one a playwright. The director is Sam Peckinpah, whose best-known film is *Ride the High Country*. In
an interview in *Film Quarterly* (Winter 1963–64), he was
asked, "Do you feel there's any common thread running
through your work?" He answered:

> If you mean message, no—leave that to Army Special Serv-
> ices. But up to date it seems that most of my work has been
> concerned one way or the other with outsiders, losers, loners,
> misfits, rounders—individuals looking for something besides
> security.

The first sentence is a strong reaction to the possibility of anyone's putting a simple label on his work. The second, however,
is an admission that he deals with particular kinds of people,
and the "one way or the other" suggests that the films,
through their action, embody a theme. When the young man
in *Ride the High Country* changes sides in the showdown between the man who wants to deliver the gold and the man
who wants to steal it, the external action is carried forward
and the internal action (from the young man's point of view)
reaches a climax. The action, however, has implications. Peckinpah may not be delivering a message, but he is making a
statement which contains an implied moral.

Arthur Miller is the playwright. When his play *After the
Fall*, appeared in *The Saturday Evening Post* (February 1,
1964), he contributed a foreword which begins, "This play
is not 'about' something; hopefully, it is something." One
hears echoes of Archibald MacLeish. In his second sentence,
however, Miller, in trying to tell us what the play "is," tells
us what it is about: "And primarily it is a way of looking at
man and his human nature as the only source of the violence
which has come closer and closer to destroying the race."
Shortly after the play's publication, in an article in *Life* (Feb-

ruary 7, 1964), Miller said, without the hedge of quotation marks, that this is "a play about the human animal's unwillingness or inability to discover in himself the seeds of his own destruction." By the end of the play, however, Quentin, the main character, seems to have made that discovery, seems to have accepted his own guilt, his own instinct for violence. Out of that knowledge, the play suggests, he will try to live so that he not blame others for his failures, so that he destroys neither them nor himself. The play, as always with Miller, has a great deal of "about" about it.

Since a play or a movie involves the choice of particular characters, the placing of them in particular situations, the putting into their mouths of particular lines, the writer is imposing some kind of order. There are implications of meaning in any arrangement of people and events; the artistic arrangement implies the statement of an idea or a theme. This is clear from the remarks of both Peckinpah and Miller, even though they begin with something very like denial. Where then is the problem? It lies in a presumed quarrel between the writer and the man in the audience. The latter is supposed to like neat, simple ideas that he can sum up quickly and comfortably, and such a summation, the writer feels, never does justice to his play. We can see this attitude in some satirical lines from N. F. Simpson's *A Resounding Tinkle*, a play about the writing of plays: "[We] do all like, naturally, to feel we've been provided with a meaning; something we can carry round with us like an umbrella for a few days." We see it also in Thornton Wilder's *The Skin of Our Teeth*, where the actress cannot stand the play she is in and cries out, "Oh—why can't we have plays like we used to have—*Peg o' My Heart*, and *Smilin' Thru*, and *The Bat*—good entertainment with a message you can take home with you?"

There are plays that give you messages to take home with you, or to carry around like an umbrella, as the first part of this chapter indicated. In most plays, however, the theme cannot be easily separated from the action, just as the action cannot be separated from the characters, or the characters from their language. The theme can be stated, and often is— by critics, by members of the audience, even by playwrights when they want to talk about the play. This is a respectable thing to do so long as the person making the statement does not imagine that in it he has given the essence of the play. The man who comes out of a performance of *Macbeth* and says, "Boy, crime does not pay," may not have made an inappropriate statement, but he has made an incomplete one.

A play—even a bad play or a simple-minded one—is a reasonably complicated work. It is a combination of theme, action and character, expressed through words, gesture, setting, props, light, sound, costume—all the elements we have examined in this book. We have had to take them separately, since that is the only way to talk about them, but the play— like any other work of art—is a joining of elements. Seeing a play is like eating a good vegetable soup. There is a certain pleasure in being able to recognize the ingredients, but the greatest pleasure comes in tasting the combination—the soup as a whole.

What to Read

The plays mentioned in the chapters of this book are there because they are examples of particular things that contribute to the making of a play. Some of them are very fine plays; some of them are quite ordinary. They are in no way a cross section of the history of drama. It would be useful to go out and read them, if only to be certain that they make the points I say they do, but if you want to approach the history of drama in a more orderly way, the suggested readings that follow can serve as a guide. I am not going to offer a traditional bibliography, with dates and publishers, because most of the plays on the list are available in a variety of editions. Any reasonably good library will have most of them. A great many of them will be available in paperback. If you want to know what you can get in paperback, go to any bookstore and consult the most recent edition of *Paperbound Books in Print*.

The divisions that follow are there because they are convenient ways of classifying drama from a historical standpoint. The suggested plays are either generally accepted as the most important for the period and the author in each case or else they are special favorites of mine. The very brief descriptions should not be taken too seriously. Summarizing a play in a sentence or two is an exercise in falsification, but even a hint of a play's subject may be of use to someone who does not know the play at all. There are two ways of approaching the list and both have merit. If you have a tidy mind, read straight through. Otherwise, read at random and, when you find a period or an author that you like, read intensively.

GREEK DRAMA

There are only a small group of Greek tragedies extant; a play a day for a month will take you almost through the lot of them. There are, of course, many translations of the Greeks, but a contemporary translation is likely to prove the most interesting. David Grene and Richmond Lattimore have edited *The Complete Greek Tragedies* for The University of Chicago Press; all of the plays are in recent translations. If you want to be more selective, concentrate on the plays that follow.

Aeschylus ORESTEIA

The Greek tragedies were written for presentation as groups of three connected plays, but this is the only trilogy that has survived. Consisting of *Agamemnon*, *The Libation Bearers*, and *The Eumenides*, the trilogy tells the story of the murder of Agamemnon and the revenging of his death with emphasis on the religious and social significance of those acts.

Sophocles OEDIPUS REX

See Chapter 3. This is the most famous of the Greek tragedies and the one that gave Aristotle his idea of what a tragic hero should be.

PHILOCTETES

In this play, Philoctetes is convinced that he should bring Achilles' bow and rejoin the Greeks, who once rejected him. It involves both the conflict between idealism and practical politics and that between private and public loyalty.

Euripides ALCESTIS

Heracles brings the heroine back from death in a play which considers the ways in which the prospect of death affects the relationships within a family. Some people take it as a sardonic comedy.

MEDEA

To punish Jason, Medea destroys their children. This is probably one of the two most famous jealousy plays ever written (*Othello* is the other).

THE TROJAN WOMEN

One of the most moving antiwar plays in the history of drama. It deals with the women who survived the fall of Troy.

There are even fewer Greek comedies than there are tragedies—eleven by Aristophanes and three by Menander.

Aristophanes THE BIRDS

A satiric fantasy in which an alliance between a discontented Athenian and the birds brings about the creation of Cloudcuckooland, a situation which lets Aristophanes make fun of most of the things he dislikes. William Arrowsmith has a new translation.

ROMAN DRAMA

Compared to the Greek drama, that of the Romans is pretty dull. It would be better to read all of the Greeks than one of the Romans. Of the latter, the comic writers—Plautus and Terence—are much the most interesting.

Plautus THE MENAECHMI

This is a farce built on the complications that follow when one twin gets confused with another. Shakespeare used it as a source for *The Comedy of Errors*.

MEDIEVAL DRAMA

The plays of this period were mostly *miracles* or *mysteries* (the names given to the retelling of the Biblical stories) or *moralities* (didactic plays making use of abstract characters). The authors are unknown.

EVERYMAN See Chapter 4. The quotation there is from John Gassner's modernization.

ITALIAN RENAISSANCE

The tragedies of this period were for the most part too intent on following models from Rome and are of very little interest. The comedies are more fun. Intricately plotted businesses involving stock characters, they seem somewhat static as we read them, but they do have satiric point and are often bawdy.

Niccolò Machiavelli MANDRAGOLA
> The usual mixture of trickery and seduction. The play has a special interest (which does not make it any better a play) because it was written by one of the most famous political philosophers who ever lived.

ELIZABETHAN AND JACOBEAN DRAMA

This is generally accepted as England's great period of drama. It had Shakespeare, after all, and that is difficult to beat. There is no point in directing anyone to this or that Shakespearean play, because presumably some English class has already done that. The sensible thing would be to read all of his plays, but not to start out with the early ones, such as the tiresome three-part *Henry VI*. My own favorites (at the moment) happen to be *Henry IV*, *Hamlet*, and *Troilus and Cressida*.
Some of Shakespeare's colleagues—notably Ben Jonson—deserve your attention.

Christopher Marlowe THE TRAGICAL HISTORY OF
DOCTOR FAUSTUS
> The name tells the story. In this version of the Faust legend, the hero is damned when he sells his soul to the devil. There are some odd slapstick scenes.

Ben Jonson VOLPONE

A schemer pretends to be ill to cheat the people who try to buy their way into his will. A harsh and funny satire on greed.

THE ALCHEMIST

Another satire on greed, this one involving some charlatans who pretend to be alchemists able to turn base metal into gold.

BARTHOLOMEW FAIR

A fine collection of hypocrites and rogues in a lively comedy which makes good use of the fair at which the action occurs.

Thomas Dekker THE SHOEMAKER'S HOLIDAY

There is a love-across-the-classes plot which turns out well for the lovers, but the play is chiefly attractive because of its main comic character, an eccentric shoemaker who becomes Lord Mayor of London.

John Webster THE DUCHESS OF MALFI

Madness, violence, family intrigue—all the ingredients of a good lurid Jacobean tragedy—and some interesting verse besides.

SPANISH DRAMA—THE GOLDEN AGE

This period is the Spanish equivalent of the English Elizabethan, and it is as rich in drama. Lope de Vega and Calderón are the two most important dramatists.

Lope de Vega FUENTE OVEJUNA

The title is the name of a village in which the peasants revolt against oppressing noblemen and are backed by their king.

Calderón THE PHANTOM LADY

A typical romantic comedy of the period in which, through much intrigue and mistaken identity, the playwright manages to declare the love and protect the honor of his characters. Edwin Honig has recently published a good translation of this and several other Calderón plays.

FRENCH CLASSIC DRAMA

This is the period which has provided the French theater with the major plays in its repertory—the tragedies of Corneille and Racine, the comedies of Molière. The comedian has always translated better than his tragic countrymen.

Pierre Corneille THE CID

Probably Corneille's best-known play. A conflict between love and duty, involving the legendary Spanish hero.

Jean Racine PHAEDRA

Racine's retelling of the Greek legend about the woman who fell in love with her stepson, which Euripides treated in *Hippolytus*. There is a new verse translation by Robert Lowell.

Molière TARTUFFE

The title character in this satire is probably the most famous hypocrite who ever walked the stage. Richard Wilbur has written a new translation in rhymed verse.

THE MISANTHROPE

The chief character in this comedy is such a harsh judge of society that he condemns himself to solitude. A satire on the antisocial as much as on society. This one, too, has been recently translated by Richard Wilbur.

RESTORATION AND EIGHTEENTH-CENTURY DRAMA

The tragedies, mostly in rhymed verse, are modeled on those of the French dramatists and deal usually with the conflict between love and honor. They are pretty trying. The comedies written during the Restoration are satirical and sometimes affectionate examinations of a society mainly preoccupied with money and sex. The eighteenth-century comedies are more sentimental, less witty, much less amusing.

William Wycherley THE COUNTRY WIFE

> A very tough-minded comedy which uses seduction to make its satirical comment on several kinds of fool.

THE PLAIN DEALER

> Based on Molière's *The Misanthrope*, this is a blunter, harsher play than the original.

John Dryden AURENG-ZEBE

> This play will do as well as any other to give you an idea of what the tragedies of the period were like. It is impossible to take it as seriously as its own century did, but it is rather fun in a bombastic way.

William Congreve THE WAY OF THE WORLD

> Probably the most famous of the Restoration comedies, rightly renowned for its wit and its style. The subject, as usual, is marriage and money.

George Farquhar THE BEAUX' STRATAGEM

> A funny and very neatly plotted comedy about two young men who set out to make their fortunes by making the right marriages.

John Gay THE BEGGAR'S OPERA

> An early musical comedy (folk opera, it was called) about London's underworld which was a political and social satire. It is best known today because it was the source of Bertolt Brecht's *The Threepenny Opera*.

Oliver Goldsmith SHE STOOPS TO CONQUER

> A pleasant comedy full of romantic intrigue, more fun for its amusing situations and lively characters than for its plot.

All the examples I have given above are English. If you want an idea of how the same kind of comedy was done in other countries look at Carlo Goldoni (perhaps *The Servant of Two Masters*) or Beaumarchais (perhaps *The Barber of Seville*) to see what the Italian and French variations were like.

ROMANTICISM

The plays of this period (late eighteenth, early nineteenth century) were mostly a reaction to the too-formal, too-rule-conscious, too-rational tragedies of the preceding century. Now, using historical subjects, the playwrights returned happily to the passions and the excesses of Elizabethan days, but added a new element: political idealism. Shelley's *The Cenci* is probably the best English example, although it has a great many shortcomings as a play.

Johann Wolfgang von Goethe EGMONT
> A tragedy about one of the leaders of the revolt of The Netherlands. Michael Hamburger has done a new translation.

Friedrich Schiller MARY STUART
> The struggle between Queen Elizabeth and Queen Mary with the Scottish queen as the heroine.

George Büchner DANTON'S DEATH
> One of the most remarkable plays ever written. The playwright uses the figures of the French Revolution to contemplate the meaning of life in a way that makes the play sound as though it had been written in 1960 rather than 1835. Most of the English versions are rather odd, but John Holmstrom's is probably as close as you will get to Büchner.

Alfred de Musset NO TRIFLING WITH LOVE
> In some translations this play is called *Camille and Perdican*. It is about a young couple whose game of love is serious, in fact fatal, to a third person.

MODERN DRAMA

This rather strange designation covers the drama from about the middle of the nineteenth century up to the present time. It includes both the growth of realistic drama and the many kinds of nonrealistic drama that turned up as reactions to realism. This is the period that most interests me, which explains why so many of the readings that my list suggests are found at this end of the time scale. Since the number of plays is greater in this category than in any of the others, I am going to divide it according to country. There are more entries for England and the United States than there are for the other countries, not because the contemporary drama here and in England is better than that on the Continent, but because I assume that the reader of this book will be particularly interested in the plays written in his own language.

SCANDINAVIA

The two most important playwrights here are Henrik Ibsen (of Norway) and August Strindberg (of Sweden). They are also two of the playwrights who had most to do with the growth of modern drama. I suggest that you read as much of Ibsen and Strindberg as you can get your hands on and that will be quite a lot since they are both well represented in paperback.

Henrik Ibsen PEER GYNT

A fantastic and wonderfully satiric chronicle play about a man who imagines he is an individual although he continually becomes whatever is expected of him.

THE WILD DUCK

A sharp look at an idealist in operation, a do-gooder who brings disaster where he intends to bring truth.

ROSMERSHOLM

A play about a man's failure to free himself of the restrictions of conventionality. See Chapter 7.

HEDDA GABLER

One of Ibsen's greatest plays. See Chapter 4 for a brief description.

THE MASTER BUILDER

A play about an aging architect which is concerned both with the struggle between age and youth and with that between artistic integrity and social conformity.

WHEN WE DEAD AWAKEN
Ibsen's last play. By this time, his characters had become less psychological, more symbolic. Again, the problem of the aging artist.

August Strindberg THE FATHER
Strindberg always saw the relationship between men and women as the battle of the sexes. In this play, the man loses.

THE DREAM PLAY
One of the earliest and most famous expressionistic plays. See Chapter 7.

RUSSIA
Very little recent Russian drama has been translated and from what we hear of it very little would be of interest to an audience outside Russia. During the nineteenth century, however, and well into the twentieth (up, say, to the 1920s), the Russian theater produced many good plays, written often by writers who were as well known for their fiction as for their drama. Chekhov is the most important.

Nikolai Gogol THE INSPECTOR GENERAL
A comedy about an impostor who imposes on a provincial town; primarily a satiric look at small-town officials. It has been translated under a variety of names, but the word *inspector* appears in most of the English titles.

Ivan Turgenev A MONTH IN THE COUNTRY
A group of people on a Russian estate reflect the frustration, boredom and jealousy that a life of compromise has inflicted on them. A Chekhov kind of play, fifty years before Chekov was writing them.

Alexander Ostrovsky THE DIARY OF A SCOUNDREL
A satirical farce, dealing as most of Ostrovsky's do with marriage and money. It has also been translated as *Even a Wise Man Stumbles.*

Anton Chekhov THE SEA GULL
  See Chapters 2 and 5.

  UNCLE VANYA
  The presence of two outsiders on the estate that the title
  character administers serves as an occasion to remind
  everyone in the play that he has not done what he wanted
  in life.

  THE THREE SISTERS
  The three girls fail to get to Moscow, which for them
  is not so much a city as the idea of a good life.

  THE CHERRY ORCHARD
  Too ineffectual to act, a family of landowners lose their
  estate and all that the cherry orchard stands for. See Chapter 8.

Maxim Gorki THE LOWER DEPTHS
  Gorki puts a collection of the poor, the hungry, and the
  sick into a cheap lodging area to give a picture of poverty
  and its effects on men.

GERMANY

It was in Germany that a great many of the technical innovations
in theatrical production were developed. Except for the period
under the Nazis, the country has always produced playwrights
who have had an influence beyond the German borders. The
drama of the 1950s and 1960s, for instance, is heavily marked—
both in the production and in the writing—by the work of the
late Bertolt Brecht, many of whose plays are now available in
English translation.

Frank Wedekind THE MARQUIS OF KEITH
  The protagonist is one of theater's most impressive con
  men. He is no match for the conventional world, which
  outtricks but never defeats him.

Arthur Schnitzler THE GREEN COCKATOO
  A one-act play, set during the French Revolution, which
  is really a satirical examination of truth and illusion.

Carl Sternheim THE SNOB
> A satirical look at a man's economic and social success and at the society in which he achieved it.

Georg Kaiser FROM MORN TO MIDNIGHT
> A good example of a German expressionist play for the period before World War I. This one, about a bank cashier, is about the way a man can be depersonalized by work that is all routine.

Bertolt Brecht A MAN'S A MAN
> A satirical play about how a man's personality can be changed by the demands society makes on him. Incidentally, an antiwar play.

> THE THREEPENNY OPERA
> Brecht uses Gay's *The Beggar's Opera* to write his own satire on the relation between crime and business. Music by Kurt Weill. It is important to listen to the music. There are recordings in German and English (in Marc Blitzstein's translation).

> GALILEO
> Brecht uses his own version of the historical figure to write a play about the pressures of society on the artist. See Chapter 9.

> THE CAUCASIAN CHALK CIRCLE
> An old legend retold, to make Brecht's point about a world in which the good things should go to those who use them properly.

Friedrich Duerrenmatt THE VISIT
> A satire by a Swiss playwright on guilt in society in which a village destroys a man for money. The translation by Patrick Bowles is the best.

Max Frisch BIEDERMANN AND THE FIREBUGS
> A harsh fantasy about responsibility in which the protagonist, protesting his innocence, gives shelter and com-

fort to the men who burn his house down. Frisch, too, is Swiss.

FRANCE

Although the French produced some of the early realistic plays, it is the intellectual comedies, whether dressed as myth or as exercises in the absurd, that constitute their most important contributions to modern drama.

Georges Courteline THE COMMISSIONER

A harsh and funny farce in which a domineering police commissioner is beaten by his own methods.

Jean Cocteau THE INFERNAL MACHINE

A retelling of the Oedipus story which mixes contemporary psychology and satire with respect for the Greek myth.

Jean Giraudoux TIGER AT THE GATES

The French title of this play is *The Trojan War Will Not Take Place*. It is an ironic look at the attempts on both sides to avoid that war.

THE MADWOMAN OF CHAILLOT

The title character and her friends rid the world of greed and destructiveness in a fairy story that is a strong satire on society.

Michel de Ghelderode PANTAGLEIZE

Ghelderode, a Belgian playwright, called his play "a farce to make you sad." Its title hero is a kind of fool whose innocence carries him through much danger but which cannot save him in the end.

Jean Anouilh THIEVES' CARNIVAL

A farce about a band of ineffectual thieves which is, as always with Anouilh, a play about innocence in a corrupting world. See Chapter 4.

THE WALTZ OF THE TOREADORS

One of the several plays Anouilh wrote about General St. Pé, a character who seems to embody so much that is both sad and foolish about human beings.

Jean-Paul Sartre THE FLIES

In this version of the *Oresteia*, Orestes has become an existential hero. If you don't know what that is, you will when you get to the end of the play.

Eugène Ionesco THE CHAIRS

Ionesco, the most famous of the French dramatists of the absurd, is best in his one-act plays. This is my favorite, but *The Bald Soprano* and *The Lesson* are also good examples of his work.

THE REST OF EUROPE

Although there are occasional playwrights (the Hungarian Ferenc Molnár is an example) who gain world-wide reputations, the dramatic literature of the countries other than those listed above has not been widely translated into English. The two exceptions are Italy and Spain, a number of whose playwrights are available to us. I did not list those countries separately because I am going to suggest the work of only one playwright from each country—Pirandello of Italy and Lorca of Spain.

Luigi Pirandello RIGHT YOU ARE! (IF YOU THINK SO)

Also called *It Is So! (If You Think So)*, the play gives two conflicting and apparently true versions of the same family situation. See Chapter 6.

SIX CHARACTERS IN SEARCH OF AN AUTHOR

Pirandello's most famous examination of the problem of illusion and reality, of artistic truth and falsity. Six characters break in on a play rehearsal and try to dictate how their story shall be told.

Federico García Lorca THE SHOEMAKER'S PRODIGIOUS WIFE

A folk comedy which the author calls "a violent farce."

BLOOD WEDDING
Taking his material from a newspaper story about a murder, Lorca has used poetic imagery, verse, and symbolic characters to convert the incident into a play about people caught in a destructive but inescapable passion. See Chapter 4.

ENGLAND
George Bernard Shaw is the best and most important of the modern English dramatists. The few plays of his listed below are only a small sampling; it would be better to read all of his work. The list contains Irish as well as English playwrights.

Oscar Wilde THE IMPORTANCE OF BEING EARNEST
The funniest play in the English language, it kids everything from popular theater to popular prejudices.

George Bernard Shaw ARMS AND THE MAN
By contrasting his professional-soldier hero with a conventionally heroic amateur, Shaw makes a hash of romantic notions about war and love.

CAESAR AND CLEOPATRA
The most glamorous woman in history becomes a petulant schoolgirl in this very serious comedy about the education of rulers.

MAN AND SUPERMAN
Shaw turns the familiar girl-traps-boy play into a fable about the life force. The third-act dream, in which the implications are discussed amusingly, is sometimes performed separately as *Don Juan in Hell*.

MAJOR BARBARA
This is probably the play in which Shaw most effectively combines his philosophic and social ideas with a dramatic story—one in which the heroine loses and regains her faith. See Chapter 5.

HEARTBREAK HOUSE
A collection of likable and ineffectual people seen on the eve of World War I. Shaw's pained comment on the failure of his society to prevent war.

SAINT JOAN
Joan as one of the Shavian geniuses in a world not ready for her.

THE SIMPLETON OF THE UNEXPECTED ISLES
One of Shaw's late, fantastic plays. A version of the last judgment in which all the useless people disappear.

Granville Barker THE VOYSEY INHERITANCE
An intellectual comedy in which the hero's becoming a swindler is a sign of his strength. Barker is Chekhov's equal in the use of dialogue.

THE MADRAS HOUSE
An examination of the way the relations between the sexes are dictated by economics and social convention. See Chapter 3.

William Butler Yeats AT THE HAWK'S WELL
A poetic play in which the central symbol is a well, the water of which is supposed to bring eternal life. The play is designed so that its climactic moment is a dance.

John Millington Synge THE PLAYBOY OF THE WESTERN WORLD
A comedy about a young man who becomes the hero that everyone takes him to be. See Chapter 5.

RIDERS TO THE SEA
A very stark one-act play in which the last of the heroine's sons drowns.

Sean O'Casey JUNO AND THE PAYCOCK
O'Casey calls his play a tragedy because Juno must suffer the loss of her son and the breaking up of her family, but

he uses the comedy of the "paycock" as ironic comment on the serious story. See Chapter 4.

THE PLOUGH AND THE STARS

Once again the mixture of the comic and the serious, this time in a play about the Easter Rebellion of 1916. The comic figures finally become more serious than the serious characters.

W. Somerset Maugham THE CIRCLE

A very neat comedy in which the new generation makes the same mistake and/or romantic commitment that the earlier one made.

Noël Coward BLITHE SPIRIT

A batty medium and a couple of wisecracking ghosts in one of the best English farces ever written.

T. S. Eliot MURDER IN THE CATHEDRAL

A poetic drama about the nature of martyrdom which has Thomas Becket as its protagonist.

THE COCKTAIL PARTY

A play about man's relationship to God and his fellow men disguised as a drawing-room comedy. In verse. See Chapter 5.

Christopher Fry THE LADY'S NOT FOR BURNING

A comedy in verse in which the heroine escapes burning as a witch and the hero fails to get himself hanged. See Chapter 4.

Dylan Thomas UNDER MILK WOOD

Originally written for radio, the play describes with beauty and wit a Welsh town and its inhabitants from dawn to night.

Enid Bagnold THE CHALK GARDEN

A comedy of ideas pretending to be a drawing-room comedy in which the heroine saves a girl from the destructive care of her grandmother. See Chapter 5.

John Osborne LOOK BACK IN ANGER
>The play that gave the term "angry young man" to much
of the English literature written right after World War
II. About a self-pitying young man who divides his time
between abusing his wife and denouncing his society.

LUTHER
>Osborne uses his own version of Martin Luther to examine
the social consequences of personal rebellion.

Samuel Beckett WAITING FOR GODOT
>Beckett could have been listed under France since his plays
were first written in French. This one, in which two men
wait for Godot, who does not come, is about hope in a
hopeless world. See Chapter 7.

ENDGAME
>Four people acting out the end of everything. See Chap-
ter 6.

Harold Pinter THE BIRTHDAY PARTY
>Pinter uses a very real boardinghouse and very specific
characters in a play that describes the generalized and un-
certain fears that assail men.

UNITED STATES
Most of the American plays written during the nineteenth century are readable only as history. Although there were a few
interesting playwrights writing in the period between 1890 and
World War I, modern drama did not really come into its own
in America until the 1920s. Our most important playwrights are
Eugene O'Neill, Thornton Wilder, Arthur Miller, and Tennessee Williams.

Eugene O'Neill THE EMPEROR JONES
>An expressionist play in which the hero, under intense
pressure, reverts to the primitive. See Chapter 9.

DESIRE UNDER THE ELMS
A triangle play involving a father, a son, and a stepmother as much concerned with desire for land as with any other kind of desire.

THE ICEMAN COMETH
A murderer attempts to convert a group of bums in a play about the comforts of illusion.

LONG DAY'S JOURNEY INTO NIGHT
O'Neill's best play about family life. A study of the strange mixture of love, guilt, and accusation that holds four people together.

George Kelly THE SHOW-OFF
A comedy in which the big-mouthed title character actually pulls off a profitable deal. A wry comment on American success.

Elmer Rice THE ADDING MACHINE
An expressionist satire on the stifling routine of ordinary life. The hero's name is Mr. Zero, which should give you an idea.

E. E. Cummings HIM
A funny expressionist play which defies a summary sentence although the conflict between the practical woman and the imaginative man is the structure that holds the satiric bits together.

S. N. Behrman THE SECOND MAN
A sophisticated comedy whose hero is too intellectually aware of himself to become emotionally involved in any situation.

Maxwell Anderson WINTERSET
A verse drama based vaguely on the Sacco-Vanzetti case in which, as so often with Anderson, the hero and heroine choose to die rather than to be corrupted by the world. See Chapter 8.

Clifford Odets AWAKE AND SING
> A Bronx family during the depression. At the end, the son sets out, somewhat vaguely, to make a better world. See Chapter 5.

THE COUNTRY GIRL
> A play about an alcoholic actor's attempt to get back on his feet in which the best thing is the way he uses his wife's attempts to help him. See Chapter 7.

Lillian Hellman THE LITTLE FOXES
> Portrait of a greedy Southern family at the turn of the century which becomes an implicit indictment of capitalism.

William Saroyan MY HEART'S IN THE HIGHLANDS
> A one-act play which, as always with Saroyan, uses a collection of slightly eccentric characters to emphasize that life, however unpleasant, is good.

Thornton Wilder OUR TOWN
> A play in which the author dispenses with scenery in an attempt to show that the details of small-town American life belong to all men not to one place or time.

THE SKIN OF OUR TEETH
> Man's history in brief in an expressionist comedy which shows man surviving natural and man-made disasters— the Ice Age, the Flood, war.

Arthur Miller DEATH OF A SALESMAN
> A man, a failure by his own standards, dies still believing in the dream of success that he has accepted. See Chapters 6 and 8.

THE CRUCIBLE
> A play about the Salem witch-hunts which is concerned both with the town's hysteria and the hero's sense of integrity.

Tennessee Williams **THE GLASS MENAGERIE**
A play in which the three main characters use various kinds of illusion to escape the harshness of the real world. See Chapters 7 and 8.

A STREETCAR NAMED DESIRE
The heroine of this play, unable to sustain the illusions that give her a little comfort, is driven by violence into madness. See Chapter 8.

Carson McCullers **THE MEMBER OF THE WEDDING**
An imaginative twelve-year-old girl, a Negro cook, and a boy of seven carry on two acts of remarkable conversation before violence and death break into this play about disconnection and loneliness.

Edward Albee **THE ZOO STORY**
A one-act play in which one man forces another to kill him.

Arthur Kopit **OH DAD, POOR DAD, MAMMA'S HUNG YOU IN THE CLOSET AND I'M FEELIN' SO SAD**
A funny play which take a satiric look at two kinds of American women.

One of the most interesting kinds of American theater is the musical comedy. I have listed none here, but it might be valuable to read Arthur Laurents' *West Side Story*, or Lillian Hellman's *Candide*, but only if you can listen to the recording of Leonard Bernstein's music at the same time. In musicals, it is the combination that counts.

INDEX